Anna Lo was born in Hong Kong and, after marrying a Belfast-born journalist, settled to live in Northern Ireland in 1974. She worked as a freelance contributor for the BBC Chinese Service and as a secretary for the World Service in Belfast before taking a break to raise her two sons. She returned to work as a part-time interpreter for the Chinese community but later went to university and qualified as a social worker, going on to work in social services and with the charity, Barnardo's. In 1997 she was appointed Director of the Chinese Welfare Association and has been at the forefront of the promotion of racial equality ever since. In 2000 she was awarded an MBE in recognition of her work in this field. She joined the Alliance Party in 2006 and was elected as a member of the Northern Ireland legislative assembly in March 2007, making history as the first China-born parliamentarian in Europe. She served two terms and retired in March 2016.

Anna Lo

The Place I Call Home

I Call Home

From Hong Kong to Belfast – *My Story*

To: Janny

Best wishes,

Anna

2018

·THE·
BLACK
STAFF
PRESS

First published in 2016 by Blackstaff Press
4D Weavers Court
Linfield Road
Belfast BT12 5GH

With the assistance of
The Arts Council of Northern Ireland

LOTTERY FUNDED

Typeset by KT Designs, St Helens, England

Printed and bound by Martins the Printers, Berwick-upon-Tweed

A CIP catalogue for this book is available from the British Library

ISBN 978-0-85640-985-1

www.blackstaffpress.com

To all my family and friends who have
helped to make Northern Ireland
the place I call home.

Contents

1

The Wai Family

I always knew my mother, Wai Kam-Ping, came from a wealthy family that had gone into decline, but I knew little more than that. She was always very reluctant to talk about her family background. I heard only snippets of past events and had almost no inkling of the myths, intrigue and possibly even murder in the history of the Wai family, going back to the mid-nineteenth century. I only really learned about my own background in a visit I made to Hong Kong in 2008, when I delved into the family history with my fourth uncle, my mother's younger brother, who told me some amazing stories about our ancestors. Some of the events and long-observed traditions resonated with Ireland's past as well as with modern-day China.

Like the Irish, the Chinese have been renowned for emigration to many different parts of the world for centuries and have brought their culture and influence wherever they have gone. My great-grandfather, Wai Lo-Yit, hailed from Toishan, a county in the Guangdong province of southern China. From there, in the mid-nineteenth century, just as one million Irish peasants left Ireland for America during the potato famine of the 1840s, young people began to emigrate to countries such as Malaysia, Indonesia and even the USA. During a period of famine in the 1860s, Wai Lo-Yit set off with some other young men for Hawaii, known in Chinese as the 'Sandalwood Mountain', some seven thousand miles from Toishan, in search of a better life. During the nineteenth century, labourers were imported from China to work on sugar plantations in Hawaii and many became merchants after their contracts expired. The ethnic makeup in Hawaii had always been diverse and remains so now – but the state's 1900 census showed that 56 per cent of its population were Chinese. Honolulu's Chinatown is one of the oldest Chinatowns in the USA.

Wai Lo-Yit prospered in Honolulu, setting up an import/export firm that shipped goods between Honolulu and China. Some years later he returned to China as a wealthy man and moved to the capital, Beijing, to live in an ostentatious mansion with a massive garden where, legend had it, people spotted Chinese fairytale foxes. However, he later moved back to Toishan, having established businesses in Beijing, Shanghai, Guangdong, Hong Kong and Honolulu.

After the death of his first wife, with whom he had two sons, Wai Lo-Yit married my great-grandmother. Together they produced another three sons and two daughters. My grandfather, Wai Kun-Hin, was born in Toishan in 1890, the fourth child in the family.

My great-grandfather, it seemed, also had a number of concubines. Indeed, during his lifetime it was customary for well-heeled men to have many concubines to show off their wealth and virility. Although there is no record that Wai Lo-Yit's concubines had any children, it is likely that they did. During the Qing dynasty (1644–1912) a concubine had a much-inferior status in the household to the wife, and the son of a concubine would never be equal to a son born of marriage. Nonetheless, producing a son could gain a concubine a modicum of long-term security for herself. Daughters, on the other hand, were deemed not only worthless in themselves, but also a financial burden – a prosperous father would have to provide a handsome dowry in order for a daughter to marry someone of the same social standing.

Girls born to my great-grandfather's concubines were rumoured to have been either smothered to death at birth or taken away to be reared by the concubine's family; my great-grandfather would have been told that they had been stillborn.

It is difficult to ascertain whether Wai Lo-Yit really was ignorant of this practice or whether he turned a blind eye to it. After all, a large number of daughters requiring expensive dowries would have dissipated his fortune. Favouring boys over girls is ingrained in Chinese culture and, in fact, still happens today. In modern China we see the unintended consequences of the state's decades-long one-child policy, which has sadly resulted in many female infants being abandoned or aborted.

I remember my mother mentioning that one of their old servants would tell the stories of Wai Lo-Yit's concubines and would attribute the fact that the family fortune had dwindled in the hands of the sons of one generation to karma – payback for the killing of so many innocent female babies. I have often wondered whether that was the reason why the Wai family never talked about my great-grandfather. Were they ashamed of him because he had been responsible for these deaths and thus for the family's decline? Some western economists have analysed why so many thriving Chinese business empires failed when fathers passed them on to their sons. They concluded that the fault rested in the unwillingness of fathers to trust outsiders, despite the fact that others would have been more able than their sons to maintain and expand their established enterprises.

Whatever else happened in his lifetime, I admire Wai Lo-Yit's pioneering spirit and entrepreneurship. He turned himself from a young peasant in a fishing village to an enormously successful businessman. It took a great deal of determination and hard graft to build a new life in a foreign country – as I found out for myself a century later.

At the turn of the twentieth century, my grandfather, Wai Kun-Hin, was sent to a British-run boarding school in Hong Kong, Saint Stephen's College, with the intention that he should later attend the University of Hong Kong, one of the most prestigious higher-education colleges in east Asia at the time. He was also expected to take over the Hong Kong branch of the business from my great-grandfather.

Wai Kun-Hin married Chan Fong-Lan, an ethnic Chinese Malaysian woman from a wealthy family that had business connections with my great-grandfather. They married in China, both aged sixteen, as was the custom at the time. Apparently, they were of the same height when they married, but my grandfather shot up in his late teens and was eventually a head taller than his petite wife. They produced six daughters and five sons, of whom two were lost in infancy. My mother was the fifth daughter.

My grandfather was an imposing figure. He was tall and broad, with big, round eyes, a large nose (which turned red in later years) and a white moustache – features more common to a Eurasian in general than to a smaller southern Chinese person. As was the case in many colonial areas of the world, there was a tendency to view a European look as desirable, and he was probably considered really handsome in his day. My mother and her siblings were very good looking and well built. They all inherited his slightly western appearance, with sharp features and pale skin. By this time western influence – from Hollywood movies to popular music and fashion – was pervading Hong Kong and European features were seen as even more attractive. Western tourists in Hong Kong often mistook my mother for an expatriate and asked her for directions – which embarrassed her, as she did not speak English.

At nineteen, my grandfather inherited all of my great-grandfather's properties and his tea and coal businesses in Hong Kong. The other brothers took over the businesses in Beijing, Shanghai and Honolulu. The youngest son, who graduated in western medicine from a medical college in Guangdong, established a private hospital in Toishan. He later died as a result of opium addiction, which was rife in China at the time. People had no idea how harmful the drug was back then and it was fashionable for middle-class men to visit opium dens in their neighbourhoods.

My grandfather stayed in Hong Kong but was not interested in the mundane business of tea and coal retail. The management of the businesses was handed to staff; the shops gradually went into decline and eventually closed. He invested in new ventures and later on switched his attention to speculation in the volatile gold market, but unfortunately lost most of his wealth this way. His preoccupation with gold was evident in the fact that he included the word *kam*, which means gold, in the names of all his daughters. My mother's name was Kam-Ping. She hated it – to her, it was vulgar.

My grandfather died in Hong Kong in 1972, aged eighty-two. Apparently, all his brothers died before him and it is believed that the Wai business empire dissolved in the hands of the five sons in their lifetime. However, even if their commercial interests had lasted until 1949, it is likely that the communist regime in China would have taken control of them.

My maternal grandmother was born in Kuala Lumpur in Malaysia, the youngest in a large family. At the age of six or seven she left Malaya on board a ship to Shanghai to avoid her family subjecting her to the cruel custom of foot-binding. Even though the family had left China, they had upheld that awful custom, which had ruined the lives of millions of Chinese women for hundreds of years. However, when the new Republic of China was established in 1912 it banned foot-binding and her oldest brother, who had moved to Shanghai, conspired with their siblings to free her from the grip of the torturous practice. They arranged for my grandmother to disguise herself as a boy and, accompanied by her maid dressed as a man pretending to be her father, to escape to the new state by sea.

The same brother had a business connection with the Wai family, which is how my grandmother later came to marry my grandfather. She was a well-known beauty, genteel and cultured, and the daring escape demonstrated the steely streak in her character. I remember her always dressed immaculately in a traditional Chinese silk dress known as a *cheongsam*. Her sleek black hair was always tied up in a bun, decorated with a carved comb or fresh flowers; her face was always powdered and her eyebrows pencilled in. In contrast to my grandfather, who always wore a stern expression, she was always smiling. She took me to my first outdoor Cantonese opera when I was about five. I still have a vague memory of the actors in their colourful costumes and headgear on the stage.

However, having been brought up in a wealthy family employing an array of servants and nursemaids, my grandmother was not one bit domesticated and had little interest in the day-to-day care of her children. According to my aunts, she was happy spending most of her time playing *mah-jong* with friends and attending operas, leaving the responsibility of managing the home and supervising her family to the servants and my eldest aunt, her first-born, who commanded the deep respect and devotion of her younger siblings even into their adulthood. Nevertheless, we were all fond of my sweet-natured, gentle grandmother.

Things were very different for my mother, who could rarely afford paid help. Unlike her own mother, she devoted all her time and effort to rearing her children and making sure her home remained a loving environment in which we could grow and develop happily.

2

The Lo Family

My father, Lo Ping-Fai, born in 1908, was the only child of his family. My paternal grandfather died when Lo Ping-Fai was in his late twenties – my mother never met him. This grandfather originally came from a town in Guangdong called 'The Three Waters'. As a herbalist, he gathered wild plants and travelled throughout southern China to sell them as medicines, eventually settling in Hong Kong in the late nineteenth century. My great-uncle was also a herbalist and used to give us prescriptions for bags of dried plants and mysterious dried insects from the Chinese medicine shops for our ailments. My mother would brew them in a clay pot for hours until they were a thick, black soup, which tasted absolutely foul. We had to swallow it down as fast as we could; then, if we were lucky, we were rewarded with a sweet.

Our paternal grandmother, whom we called Ah-Mah, was from a peasant background. She was illiterate and had escaped the custom of foot-binding because she had been brought up to work in the fields. Ah-Mah lived with us until she died, aged ninety-three – it was traditional for a widowed mother to live with her eldest son until death. Ah-Mah was made of hardy stock. She could not have been more different from my maternal grandmother, who was genteel and refined. She was hardly ever ill and hardly ever complained about anything, although she suffered from cataracts and had very poor eyesight late in her life. Nonetheless, she was always the first person to get up to make Chinese tea in the morning. She helped my mother with the housework, as well as looking after the grandchildren. Amazingly, the two women got on really well, sharing respect for each other and love for my father, to whom they were both devoted.

Unusually, both my parents were born in Hong Kong, in contrast to the majority of the population of the British colony, who came there to seek refuge from communist rule in China in 1949. My father, although small in stature, was sharp in intellect. He received a British education in Hong Kong's first government grammar school, Queen's College, and graduated with flying colours, including colony-wide awards. However, because his family was poor, he had to leave school to join the civil service. He continued to study accountancy at night.

He and two other young civil servants began to court my mother and her two older sisters, who were renowned for their beauty and refined family background. These three civil servants eventually married the Wai sisters. My mother was only twenty, ten years younger than my father, when they married.

Father rose rapidly within the Treasury and was in charge of a small team of officials during World War II, when the Hong Kong government retreated to Sichuan in mainland China. The job carried a lot of responsibility and he hoped that by taking it he would advance his career when he returned to the colony. Sichuan is a mountainous area and the cold and damp environment, coupled with a dense population, provided ideal conditions for the spread of tuberculosis. Being from the warm climate of Hong Kong and unused to the cold, my father contracted the deadly disease towards the end of the war in Sichuan. Although he survived, it made a dramatic difference to his life and, later, to the lives of his children.

On their return to Hong Kong in 1945, my parents found themselves faced with a housing shortage – hundreds of thousands of people were leaving mainland China for fear of a looming civil war. Along with their two very young sons and my father's mother, they moved in with my maternal grandparents, the Wai family. The stay was probably envisaged as a temporary measure until they found somewhere else. But demand for housing reached unprecedented levels when Mao Tse-Tung established the People's Republic of China in 1949 and millions more Chinese people fled to Hong Kong to escape communism.

When my father recovered from his bout of tuberculosis, the Treasury offered him a job that would place his former subordinates above him. Being a proud man, he turned down the offer. The civil service also refused to grant him a pension on the grounds that he had been offered a return to work, albeit in a position that he had not found satisfactory. Being able to read and write English, Father petitioned the then-governor of Hong Kong, Sir Alexander Grantham (1947–57), who intervened and decided that the civil service was breaking the law in denying him his entitlement to a pension. The governor of Hong Kong ruled supreme in the colony and it must have been quite unusual for an ordinary citizen even to write to him at that time. For the governor to take action on behalf of a medically retired civil servant would have been unheard of.

Father then went into business, setting up a small factory making plastic signage. The factory was named Man-Wah, after me (Man-Wah is my Chinese name), but it was not a successful venture. He also got into partnership with others to export goods from Hong Kong to mainland China. This was a lucrative trade but a risky one, as China was under communist rule and had a strict closed-door policy. They were lucky for a while, but eventually the Chinese authorities detected and confiscated their ship and its cargo. My father and his partners got into serious debt. Facing the prospect of jail and out of desperation, he took my eldest brother, David, who was about ten years of age, and went into hiding for nearly two years in Macau, a Portuguese colony near Hong Kong, until the coast was clear.

When I was born in 1950, the shipping business was at its peak and we were wealthy. My mother was chauffeur driven in our black Austin to Queen Mary Hospital for my birth, a fact that Mother and Ah-Mah mentioned to me more than a few times. However, the calamity of losing the ship soon after my birth turned our financial circumstances upside down. We faced near-destitution and were probably only saved by handouts from the Wai family. Those older relatives who still believed in Chinese superstition called me the one with the 'bad foot', a bringer of bad *feng shui* (that is, misfortune) to the family. I had been born not only in the year of the tiger but also in the hour of the dragon. Ah-Mah remarked that this was not auspicious – that particular zodiac alignment was too rough a ride for a girl.

As a baby, I was oblivious to this and I do not recall anyone pointing the finger at me later – but I think I did have a sense, somehow, that I was not Ah-Mah's favourite grandchild. One of my aunts told me when I was a bit older that my grandmother had hardly ever held me when I was little because of the superstition.

Eventually the debts were cleared and, returning from Macau, my father got a job in the accounts department of an international shipping company, which had its office in the Hong Kong and Shanghai Bank building, one of the most prestigious buildings in the colony at the time. Father worked on an upper floor, amid honey-coloured panelled walls and hushed voices. It was always a treat to go to his office with my mother on a Saturday morning. People worked a half day on Saturdays at that time and we would sit on the plush chairs in the reception area waiting for him to finish work before going for *dim-sum* lunch in Central District. *Dim-sum* lunch in a restaurant was our favourite treat. Along the aisles between tables, waitresses would push trolleys stacked high with freshly steamed prawn dumplings, pork buns and dozens of other delicious bite-size snacks in bamboo baskets, while customers picked what they liked from them.

Father was very interested in local news and international affairs. Every evening after work he would come home with an armful of newspapers and retreat to the bedroom to read the papers all evening after dinner. Although he was a traditional family man of the day – that is, not involved in domestic chores or rearing children, which was, of course, left to the wife – he was modern in his outlook and receptive to western culture. He loved Coca-Cola, which was in vogue in the 1940s, and Hollywood movies, particularly those featuring Fred Astaire and Ginger Rogers. He excelled at ballroom dancing and, with my beautiful mother as his partner, was a ballroom-dancing champion, waltzing away in glitzy dance halls. He and Mother taught for a few years in a dance school in the front lounge of Grandfather Wai's house, thus continuing their interest in dancing and probably also boosting their income.

Father fell out with his in-laws after we moved to live with them in very crowded conditions in Wan Chai. Perhaps inevitably, given Father's westernised attitudes and lowly background, my grandfather, Wai Kun-Hin, had always looked down on him. He had been allowed to marry Mother because they had thought he had a future in the civil service. The loss of the shipping business and the interlude in Macau had not helped to smooth relations.

Famously in our family, Father made a stand against my grandparents one Chinese New Year. According to an old Chinese custom my grandfather wished to maintain, all of his children and their spouses were to line up to kneel and bow in front of grandfather and grandmother and to wish them good health and prosperity for the year to come. Father accused them of being old-fashioned and refused to kow-tow to them at this gathering. That day and, indeed, from then on, my mother went on her own with us children.

It could not have been easy for her and we, as children, felt the tension between Father and the Wai grandparents, particularly when we were living in the same house. Whilst our cousins went in and out of my grandparents' living quarters, we never set foot inside, even though Mother never actually told us not to. We were proud children.

My mother, meanwhile, was a disappointed woman. A beauty from a wealthy family, she would have expected a better life than she got. Her father had given his daughters a good education, which was not that common for that generation, although my mother and her sisters never completed their schooling. Money grew tight as Wai Kun-Hin's various business ventures failed and the gold market did not yield the gold nuggets he had hoped for – and his daughters were taken out of school. My mother could have attained a teaching qualification had she been able to complete her education.

In those days, though, a married woman with children – especially one from a good family – was not expected to earn a living. Indeed, it would have been considered a massive source of shame for her father or husband if she had to bring in money. If Mother could have worked, it would have saved us from poverty when Father fell ill and when his business went bust. But she never had the chance to have a career. I think that that was part of the reason why she had no aspiration for me to become anything more than a housewife like her.

It was unfortunate, too, that tuberculosis prevented my father from climbing the ladder in the Treasury. As an accounts clerk in the shipping company, he was poorly paid. In contrast, my mother watched her two brothers-in-law – who had been my father's friends when they had been dating the three sisters – doing well in their government jobs. Mother's eldest sister married a school inspector who rose to a senior position in the Education Department. It must have been very hard for Mother to see that they all had a comfortable lifestyle with servants and cars. Only her younger sister, my sixth aunt, was poorer than us. Her husband, too, had nearly died from tuberculosis. He had survived the dreadful disease with only one lung and had never been able to work again.

My mother worried about money the whole time we were growing up and occasionally had to borrow small sums of cash from her older sisters to tide her over until Father's next payday. As a child, I thought she looked sad sometimes and I guessed that she was envious of her well-off sisters.

Despite our hand-to-mouth existence, Mother tried to feed and clothe us as best she could and was always conscious that we should be presentable. She used to make dresses for me or alter hand-me-down clothes from our cousins so that they looked slightly different from the originals. I really appreciated this – knowing that our cousins would recognise their own discarded clothing, I hated wearing cast-off clothes to family occasions.

Mother loved reading and there were bookcases in our flat with thick volumes of translated books by Jane Austen, Thomas Hardy and some American writers. Like most of her family, she was a Taoist and would visit the Taoist temple hall in a block of flats near where we lived. My father was also a Taoist, although I am not sure if Mother converted him. For many years he would meditate in their bedroom first thing in the morning and after work, which supposedly kept his high blood pressure in check.

We children had to stay quiet while he was meditating so as not to disturb him.

My mother was a bit of a dreamer. Unfortunately, her dreams of a good life never fully materialised. Nonetheless, she was a good parent – loving and totally devoted to her children. I wish she had lived long enough to see all her children succeeding in their chosen paths. I know she would have been proud of us.

3

My Childhood

I was born in the British colony of Hong Kong in June 1950. I had three older brothers – David, Eddie and Henry – and my younger sister, Mary, came along five years after me. We all had Chinese names at birth, which are generally made up of two characters. Mine is Man-Wah (meaning 'graceful and splendid') and my sister's is Man-Lai (meaning 'graceful and beautiful'). We share the middle character because we are sisters of the same family. However, we all eventually adopted English names. By the time we went to secondary school, Hong Kong was becoming westernised and young people preferred to call each other by English names. I asked my oldest brother, David, for a suggestion. David thought about it and declared, 'You shall be named Georgiana!' Georgiana, of course, is the name of Mr Darcy's sister in Jane Austen's novel *Pride and Prejudice*, which David had studied in school. (I think he fancied himself as Mr Darcy.) In class I told my friends my chosen name but it was so cumbersome that they could never remember how to say it – and I could never remember how to spell it. So I shortened it to Anna, which actually sounds more like my Chinese name; my family at home continued to use Man-Wah.

When I was growing up in the fifties and sixties there was very little public participation in the governance of Hong Kong – there were no elections or political parties. The Hong Kong government was continually wary that if the people got involved in politics they might choose to banish colonial rule and reunite Hong Kong with China. The head of the British colony was the governor of Hong Kong, usually someone appointed from British diplomatic circles. He was utterly unknown to (and, of course, unelected by) the citizens of Hong Kong. When he did appear it was always amidst great pomp and ceremony – in a white uniform with a helmet topped with ostrich plumes, a sight totally alien to the local Chinese.

It is interesting to note that eight out of twenty-eight governors of Hong Kong came from Ireland, north and south, including the first one, Sir Henry Pottinger (1843–4), who was born in County Down. The last governor of Hong Kong, Chris Patten (1992–7), was later involved in reforming policing in Northern Ireland.

There was a brief period of unrest in Hong Kong in 1967, when I was still at school. I remember being caught up in a street disturbance between pro-China protesters and riot police firing tear gas. Little did I know then that I would see a similar kind of civil unrest later on in my life, with parallel issues of identity and sovereignty at its root.

I spent my early childhood in the Wai family home, which was situated in a quiet residential area of Wan Chai, near Happy Valley Racecourse. The house was a grand two-storey red-brick western-style building with a dozen wide brick steps leading up to a panel of laced wrought-iron and carved wooden front doors, which were never locked. The house was subdivided into apartments and my grandfather, with his much-reduced inheritance, owned half of the ground floor. At the front of their apartment was a big lounge, which was later used as a dance hall in the evenings and dance school (where my parents taught ballroom dancing) in the daytime. There was a courtyard between the front lounge and the back of the house, where we all lived. My grandparents had their own living quarters – really only one big room, with lacquered Chinese furniture and a curtained bed in one corner. We had one bedroom containing a double bed, bunk-beds for the children, a folded dining table and a few chairs. Ah-Mah slept in a bed in the corridor just outside our room.

Later on, my mother's younger sister, our sixth aunt, and her family also moved in. My grandparents had a wooden loft built above a corridor as their sleeping area. The two unmarried young uncles slept in the lounge in the front of the house, where the dance school was. There was a big kitchen and a large back yard, where hens were kept.

My earliest memory is of playing in the courtyard with my brother Henry, who is eighteen months older than me, and some cousins of similar ages. Before we moved out when I was about six years old, there were three families living under the same roof – nine adults and eleven children. Amazingly, though, we seemed to get on in relative harmony. The women spent their days cooking and sitting in the kitchen area while the children played safely in the courtyard.

However, I did once witness my aunt beating one of her sons, who was the same age as me – about four or five – for some misdemeanour, with a piece of log she picked up from the basket for the kitchen stove. He jumped from foot to foot, clutching the leg she had hit and crying for her to stop. I was shocked and angry at her brutality. My mother, having trained to be a teacher, always believed that children should not be punished physically and we had never been beaten – not even a slap. My aunt was very stressed about her husband's ill health and, like ourselves, her family was in poverty and overcrowded accommodation, so her reaction to my cousin's bad behaviour was perhaps understandable. However, I always thought that my mother deserved great credit for never taking her worries out on her children.

I loved the courtyard and still remember it well. It was lined with potted bamboo plants and other shrubs, with a stone bench along one wall. There were two walls on each side – one partitioning us from the other half of the ground floor and a taller one setting the outside boundary between our house and the building next door, which was a private kindergarten. Between the two walls were windows looking into the courtyard from the front lounge and my grandparents' living quarters. I remember pushing myself up and down and around and around the courtyard in my four-wheeled wooden toy cart, which had a rabbit's face and red handles for its ears. For the autumn moon festival, children would parade around the courtyard with lit-up lanterns of all shapes and sizes. The adults would watch them from their rattan chairs while sipping tea and eating sweet 'moon-cakes'.

On one occasion, when no one was looking after me, I got into trouble. It was one of the many Chinese festivals and the adults were busy preparing food and attending to the rituals. China has no institutionalised religion but people worship dozens of different deities at different dates in the lunar calendar. Most families also have a small wooden plaque, painted red and inscribed with their family name, to commemorate their ancestors. During death anniversaries or festivals, they place lit incense sticks, fresh flowers, food and wine in front of the plaque to remember and pay respect to forebears. (Sometimes this practice is referred to by the erroneous term 'ancestor worshipping'.)

During one of those festivals, my mother poured all the small cups of Chinese rice wine into a rice bowl after the ceremony and set it on the dining table. I was only about four years old and was fed up waiting around for dinner as the adults were occupied with the festival celebrations. I climbed up onto the chair, lifted the rice bowl and drank the whole sweet, cool bowl of rice wine. Apparently I passed out after that. All I remember was waking up with a sore head and starting to cry when I saw my brothers and parents laughing at me.

The odd mishap aside, most of my memories of living in that house with my brothers and cousins are happy ones. However, the house was reputed to be haunted and many claimed to have seen ghosts throughout the building. The Chinese believe people have either *yin* (shadowy) or *yang* (sunny) eyes. Those with *yin* eyes can see unearthly figures like ghosts. My mother and my brother Henry both had *yin* eyes and both were adamant that they had seen ghosts in the house while living there. One Chinese New Year, when I was about ten years of age, we went back to see our grandparents. One of my cousins and myself went up to the roof to watch others light and throw firecrackers onto the street.

On our way back downstairs we both saw a figure standing in the corner. It looked like a blue flame in the shape of a person. We ran down the steps double-quick, scared out of our wits. I was frightened of the dark for many, many years afterwards, until my adulthood. Henry continues still to see ghostly figures in various places, including Northern Ireland. Whenever I have been considering buying a house, Henry has been invited to inspect the place and determine whether or not it is 'clean'.

We moved to the North Point Estate when I was about six years old and my younger sister, Mary, was just a baby. It was brand-new low-rent government housing in the quiet residential town of North Point, on the north-east coast of Hong Kong Island. The estate comprised three twelve-storey buildings clustered around the seafront, with a ferry pier and terminals for buses and trams. Our new flat was in the East Block, which was the first one to be completed. It had classrooms for the local primary school on the ground floor. The other two blocks had landscaped gardens and children's play areas.

The overcrowding in my grandfather's home and our large family meant that we were able to get one of the largest flats on the first floor of the first block, before the rest of the estate was even completed. It was heavenly suddenly to have so much space – a living room, our own kitchen and bathroom (although they were compact), and three double bedrooms. The East Block was beside the sea, with a wonderful view of the harbour and a cool sea breeze in the evening. Few residents had moved in before us and the estate seemed so eerily quiet compared to the bustling Wan Chai district that, for the first few weeks, until we got used to the silence, we all went to bed as soon as it started to get dark.

With the rapid population explosion in Hong Kong caused by refugees from China, hundreds of thousands of people were forced to live in makeshift shanty towns on the hills of the island. Landslides and fires happened regularly, killing many. Our sixth aunt and her family lived in one of those shanty towns for a few years when they moved out of my grandfather's house. The Hong Kong authorities faced massive pressure to alleviate the acute housing shortage and initially built multi-storey high-rise blocks of flats with very basic facilities, the so-called 'resettlement estates', to house those in the shanty towns. They also built low-rent estates for the lower middle classes, such as the one we were moving into. These were much superior to the resettlement homes, with good design, quality construction and spacious interiors.

Henry and I were unable to start school right away as we had not enrolled early enough. Children in Hong Kong at the time started primary education at the age of six or seven and continued for six years; many parents wanted their children to get into government schools, which were free and better resourced than others. My parents decided that we could defer attendance for a year as the classes had already started and were full anyway.

When we did start, because of the large number of children enrolled, the school was split into morning and afternoon sessions. Henry went to a primary-three class from 8.30 a.m. until 1 p.m. and I attended a primary-one class from 1.30 p.m. until 6 p.m. I loved art and English language, which we started to learn in primary three. Traditionally, teachers are revered in Chinese society and, as a diligent and respectful pupil, I did not have any trouble with them. The principal, who also taught us art, often picked out my drawings for praise and put them up on the wall. She really boosted my self-esteem and began my lifelong interest in art.

Hong Kong's education system was very much based on the UK model of the time. At the end of primary six, we sat an examination for secondary-level schools, similar to the old transfer test in Northern Ireland. The most sought-after secondary-level schools were, by and large, faith schools, set up and run by Christian churches but subsidised by the government. They were generally attended by middle-class children whose parents were not Christians but wanted to send their children to a school with first-class academic results. Government schools had a good reputation and tended to be preferred by parents from lower socio-economic strata, who had less money available for extra-curricular sports and other activities often required by faith schools. There were not many such schools, so the competition for admission was fierce. Children who did not get the necessary grades went to fee-paying privately run schools – which were not like the public schools in the UK, and very often had profit as their primary goal. Many of these were of a poor standard, resulting in poor academic attainment by the students.

Henry's grades were probably good enough for a middle-ranking faith school, but he ended up in a nearby private school of indifferent quality because our older brother Eddie already studied there. Eddie had gone to a free primary school run by the Salvation Army and had not sat the all-school exam. Choosing schools for the children seemed to have been left to my mother alone, who got a bit frustrated, as she was not familiar with the range of schools available. Even though none of us went to a top-grade secondary school, we were all intelligent and hard-working students with aspirations to get the most out of our education.

I went to Shaukeiwan Technical School, a brand-new government secondary school probably aimed at working-class children who would not go on to third-level education. Girls were taught typing, book-keeping and home economics in addition to the normal curriculum, while boys learned technical drawing, carpentry and metalwork. Shaukeiwan was two districts east of the more affluent area of North Point, where we lived, but there was a direct bus from the terminal just outside our block of flats and my mother thought it would be convenient for me to go to that school.

The school building was still under construction when I started and, bizarrely, we spent our first year sharing premises with a school on the western side of the island. Most of the students lived on the other side of the island, in districts in the east. For a year, I took the tram at the crack of dawn on the North Point-Western District line, all the way from one terminus to the other. For the first week, I got travel sick on the trams but I eventually got used to the one-hour journey. I had walked down one floor from my flat to my primary-school classroom for six years, but I certainly made up for that lack of travelling that first year of my secondary education.

The decision to open the new school was clearly rushed. There was, I think, one parents' information meeting, where my mother was told what school books and stationery to bring – but the school authority had not yet designed the school uniform and we were to wear our own clothes to school to start with. I remember what I wore. My mother made a lovely suit (yes, a suit!) for me, with a little round-necked jacket and matching skirt in purple and blue checked material. I looked so smart. I got off to a good start, too. After a little test, my new teacher, Mr Lin, declared that I had the best handwriting in the class and asked me to write down all the children's names for him according to where they sat.

Looking back, it seems incredible that, whilst 99 per cent of the population were Chinese, secondary schools in the British colony of Hong Kong generally taught all subjects except Chinese literature through the medium of English. The teachers, all of whom were Chinese, spoke English in class and all of the textbooks were in English. Some of the schoolbooks were simplified or abridged versions specially adapted for Hong Kong children. But, with only elementary English taught in primary schools, it was a huge struggle for pupils to bridge the gap in their command of the language between primary level and the next. It was therefore not surprising that many young people left school without any real competence in either Chinese or English. For the first two years at least, whether it was English literature, geography, or general science, I did my homework with an English–Chinese dictionary beside my textbook. We had to speak in English in class as well, which kept us very quiet most of the time.

The school principal was a Scot, Mr Halliwell. The children were scared of him – not only because he represented the school authority but also, I suspect, because of his height and his bushy eyebrows. He towered over us, the tiny Chinese boys and girls. It was typically colonial that the whole school, made up entirely of Chinese students and teachers, always had a white headteacher who could not communicate with the children he was supposed to be in charge of.

Despite my initial reservation that it was not a grammar school, I was very happy at Shaukeiwan. The school not only gave me a decent education but also helped to build my self-confidence and self-esteem. Being poor and burdened with the perception that Mother's relatives looked down on us, I had felt a bit inferior in my early childhood, but I really shone at Shaukeiwan. I was eager to learn and absorbed knowledge like a sponge. I excelled particularly in English, art and geography. We were proud to be Shaukeiwan's pioneering first-year students.

From the beginning, I was appointed a class monitor, helping teachers with chores. Later the students elected me as a class chairperson. In fourth form I became a school prefect. Even after leaving school, my peers elected me again as the first president of the Past Pupils' Association, which is still flourishing.

I made lots of friends in school and went out and about with them a lot. Bu Siu-Fun was my best friend. She lived nearby and together we learned to ride a bicycle along a stretch of pavement beside a convent school. We hung on to its six-foot wall to balance ourselves on our bikes, which we hired for one Hong Kong dollar (about ten pence) an hour. Siu-Fun was an only child and her parents could afford to pay for swimming lessons for her. I would not have dreamed of asking my parents for tuition fees, so I went to the local library and borrowed some self-teaching manuals in order to learn the strokes. I taught myself to swim in the public swimming pool in Victoria Park near our home and I still swim regularly to this day.

According to stories in Hong Kong newspapers following my election to the Northern Ireland Assembly in 2007, I was quite forthright in speaking up for my fellow students at school. I have a limited memory of those stories, but I do remember once standing up to a teacher of Chinese literature who, I believed, did not prepare adequately for lessons. I also remember challenging my English and history teacher, Miss Cheung, about the Opium Wars. I complained that our textbook, written by an English author, only carried the British perspective – which, in my view, was not an impartial one. As a teenager with a sense of patriotism, I regarded the Opium Wars as unjust and was indignant that they were narrated with a certain bias in school history books. I actually had a great deal of respect for Miss Cheung, who brilliantly coached my fifth-form class for the school's first competition in English poetry-reading, which we won. We also won the Chinese poetry-reading competition – without any help from the Chinese-literature teacher, who had been most annoyed by my complaint against him.

In 2008 there was a fortieth-anniversary school reunion for the Shaukeiwan Technical School class of 1968 in Hong Kong. During that visit I also had the chance to make a presentation at the University of Hong Kong about my work with the Chinese community in Northern Ireland, at the request of an old classmate who has become a professor there. At the end of the talk, a student raised his hand to ask a question, speaking with a familiar Northern Irish accent. He came from my constituency of

South Belfast. Small world! That school gathering saw old friends flying in from Canada, New Zealand and the UK. Past students and teachers reminisced happily about our school. The teachers, who had all retired, must have been pleased that many of their first-year protégés had done well in academia, commerce, industry and even politics.

While I thrived at school, my siblings spent the late sixties progressing in their own lives. My oldest brother, David, left school and got a job in accounting, while studying accountancy in the evening. Eddie, the next brother, went to the Hong Kong Technical College to embark on a three-year quantity-surveying course. My parents were very proud of him. The younger siblings – particularly Henry and I, who were three and five years younger than him respectively – always looked up to Eddie.

Mary is the youngest in the family and my only surviving sister; I also had an older sister who died at the age of six months during the war, when my parents were in Sichuan. They were devastated. She was hardly ever mentioned because, I think, it was always painful to talk about losing her. However, we gathered from snippets dropped by Father and Ah-Mah that she was a beautiful baby girl who was the double of my mother, with large eyes and pale skin. When I was born I looked more like my father – with sallow skin and small, narrow eyes. I believe my father was disappointed that I did not look more like my mother and the daughter that they had lost. Being small, scrawny and shy, I really was not an attractive child in his eyes.

However, the next daughter, Mary, was as beautiful as their lost infant and Father doted on her. When Mary was born he was in his late forties and the family finances had become more stable, so not only was there more spare cash to spend on the children, but there was also more opportunity to spend quality time with them.

Father never disguised his feelings towards anyone. He resented his oldest son, David, for his lack of interest in school. He adored Eddie for being clever. He paid little attention to Henry and me, who were in the middle, with no particular talents. And there was absolutely no doubt that Mary was the apple of his eye. Perhaps he wanted to make up for lost time – he had not had much involvement in rearing us older children, having been occupied with work. Naturally, we had become closer to Mother than to him. There was no mistaking the fact that Father took great pleasure in showing off his pretty and bright little girl, Mary, everywhere. When he took us to the circus for the first time, the express purpose was to let Mary see the animals and the show. We went by tram to another district for dim-sum lunch frequently because it delighted Mary to see a chained monkey leaping about in a particular balcony on our way. He decided when Mary was about three years old that she should get a present for Christmas, like children in the west do. As the second youngest, I would also get something. That Christmas morning, when I woke up, I found an exquisite wooden money-box in the shape of a Swiss chalet at the end of my bed. It was the first and only Christmas present I received as a child. I kept it for years.

As most people in Hong Kong are not Christian, the significance of Christmas was simply a few days' holiday. There were not many festivities. On the contrary, Chinese New Year, the first day of the year according to the lunar calendar, is celebrated in abundance in China, Hong Kong and overseas amongst the Chinese diaspora. Each year we spent several days visiting relatives – first of all, those on our father's side (paternal relatives are regarded as more important than those on the maternal side); then we would visit my mother's family. Until they were banned after the riots in 1967, people were allowed to light firecrackers, large and small, which were usually thrown from balconies or rooftops onto the streets below. It used to frighten the life out of me when they exploded in front of me or right behind me while we were on our way to see relatives. The essence of the festivities is to begin the year afresh and most people – young and old – would wear something new and in red, which was deemed a lucky colour. People would bring each other fruits and share special steamed cakes, washed down by gallons of hot Chinese tea. After we wished them *kung hei fat choy*, the customary greeting for the new year, adult relatives, neighbours and friends of our parents would give us children small red envelopes containing coins or banknotes referred to as *lai see* (lucky money). We usually could not wait to get home, with our pockets full of unopened red envelopes – it was impolite to open them in front of those who had given them to us. When we eventually returned home, we would gather in our parents' bedroom, each taking a corner of their double bed, and empty all the red packets out in order to count them. I always put my 'lucky money' into my lovely money-box.

From a young age, I accepted the fact that my brothers, being older – and being sons – would get more attention from Father than me; but when my younger sister, Mary, became his favourite child, I concluded that, in fact, I was somehow less worthy of his affection. No doubt this contributed to the sense I had during my early childhood that I was inferior.

Poor Mary, although favoured by Father, was an object of jealousy for her siblings. After all, it was not her fault that she was Father's favourite. We were often less than kind to her when Father was not at home. David once stuck chewing gum in her silky dark-brown hair and on another occasion pushed shiny chocolate-egg tinfoil wrappers up her nose. I would pinch her chubby arms whenever she annoyed me.

Mother was always loving and fair to all of us. Although she adhered to the custom that the sons had priority in terms of education, as they were the future breadwinners, she and I had a special bond. My three brothers were protective and clearly fond of me and I adored them, particularly David and Eddie, my two eldest brothers, who were ten and five years older than me respectively. I knew that they often spoke up for me and complained that Father spoilt Mary.

In my fifth year in school, things came to a head. Mary sat her primary-school leaving examination in early summer in 1968, about a fortnight before the start of my secondary-school leaving examinations. Her exam was just for one morning and, that same afternoon, a big cardboard box arrived as a surprise reward for her. It was our first television set – which we had all longed for – and everyone was thrilled. Mother was concerned that it might distract me from my revision, but it was too late. We could not send it back.

The television blared from late afternoon to late evening. Even though our three-bedroom flat was spacious by Hong Kong standards, it was hardly enormous, and the living room opened straight onto the bedrooms. I could hear the sound pounding through the thin walls incessantly. And, of course, when I knew my whole family were glued to the screen, I wanted to watch the programmes too. During the weeks of revision and examinations, I adopted a strategy that I had often used before for last-minute preparation before school tests. I went to bed early, about 9 p.m., and got up at 5 a.m., when there was peace and quiet. However, I rarely got to sleep early as the noise of the television kept me awake until late. Even though Mother ordered that the television volume should be turned down when I went to bed, most of the time I lay awake, frustrated that I could not get to sleep. The last exam was a Chinese-literature paper for which we had to write an essay using ink and a brush. I still remember the title – 'The Value of Education'. I was exhausted by the lack of sleep and fed up with revising at the crack of dawn. I struggled to finish the paper and, by the end, could not have cared less whether I did well or not.

When the examination results came through, I did not do as well as I should have, although I did as well as any of my brothers. Not only did I fail mathematics (that was not a huge surprise, as it had always been my weakest subject) but I also failed Chinese literature. No one fails Chinese literature – it is our own mother tongue and supposedly easy to pass. It was utterly inexcusable and I really regretted my own lack of effort that last morning, when I could not wait to get out of the examination hall to go home to get some sleep. What's more, my family teased me for many years for this 'folly'. My geography and English teachers expressed their disappointment in my grades and I hung my head in shame. Eddie was still in the technical college at this time and Henry was doing his A levels. Mother said that I had to start looking for a clerical job, since I already had typing and book-keeping qualifications. I would not be going to university.

There were only two universities in Hong Kong in the sixties for a population of five million: the Chinese University and the University of Hong Kong. The English-based University of Hong Kong was more prestigious and most people wanted to get in there, but competition was fierce. Many better-off families sent their children overseas to universities in the USA, Canada or the UK.

To be truthful, I had not realistically anticipated the chance of a university education but I certainly did not expect to go straight out of school into a job. I could have enrolled for an art course in one of the further-education colleges. I had won prizes in school and my artwork was always on display in the classroom and school hall. My brothers protested on my behalf and – out of guilt, I guessed – my father reluctantly told my mother to let me know that if I wished I could repeat a year and try to get better results. But money was still tight and I knew Mother wanted me to contribute to the family income. To pacify me, she also said something that, I suppose, summed up parental aspirations for daughters in Hong Kong in those days: girls should not be too clever – otherwise, how would they find a husband?

This was the first time I had really felt a sense of injustice. My older brothers were all given opportunities for further education.

My results, though not as good as they should have been, were no worse than theirs, yet I was pushed out to earn money to help to finance their studies. I felt let down and the fact that I was prevented from going on to further education left me with a big chip on my shoulder. I understood the family's economic constraints but I realised, too, that my parents had no career aspirations for me because I was just a daughter.

Compliantly, however, I got a job in an offsite administration office for a factory based in the New Territories, where many such factories had been set up in the fifties and sixties. The factory made cheap plastic goods. Its office, stuffed with samples of plastic flowers and toys, was in a run-down office block in the Kowloon Peninsula. I had to take a ferry, then a bus, to get to and from work, in the summer heat of thirty-five degrees Celsius for a measly monthly wage of about £25. I gave a third of this to Mother. Apart from me, there was only the sour-faced manager in the cramped office. Probably knowing I would not stick with the job for long, he hardly ever talked to me.

In the end, I was there for three months; then I got a junior clerical position with the Hong Kong Telephone Company in a skyscraper in Hong Kong Island's Central District. Two of my close friends from school had joined the company just before me, but they were in accounts. I was sent to the general office as a junior clerk, dealing with administration for telephone connections and customer enquiries. My colleagues were friendly and helpful and there were many school-leavers like me, trying to work their way up, although many remained in the same post for years and years. I knew it would take me a long time to climb the ladder, but I only stayed for two years.

After that I joined the Hong Kong and Shanghai Bank, which is technically the central bank in Hong Kong, as a cashier in its headquarters in Central District. This was a job with higher pay and better prospects for promotion. Father still worked in the shipping company a few floors up in the same, iconic building, but we never travelled to work together. He liked to leave the house early for *dim-sum* breakfast in a restaurant near home.

We cashiers sat behind the counter dealing with customers for most of the day and sorted money in the basement after we closed the counter at 3 p.m. The bank was situated in the commercial hub of Hong Kong and we would have both Chinese and non-Chinese customers who worked in the nearby offices of international companies. Usually, customers were patient while they waited to be served but, at times, the European customers complained the queues were too long – and usually got quicker attention as a result. The cashiers were generally a bit wary of foreign customers, who seemed more demanding than Chinese ones.

Most senior staff, both in the Hong Kong Telephone Company and the Shanghai Bank, were English-speaking expats – mostly from the UK but sometimes from the USA, Canada or Australia. It was the same across the board in government departments and international companies in Hong Kong. All top civil servants and executives were English, American or Australian. Most westerners socialised with their own people and Chinese people did the same. The majority of westerners lived in the Mid-Levels, up the hills of Hong Kong. They had better jobs and were probably better qualified, but Chinese people very often suspected that westerners were promoted faster than their Chinese counterparts.

The official language of the British colony was English. There was always a warning on official documents that, if there was a Chinese translation, it was the English version that had primacy. Even though only 2 per cent of the population of Hong Kong at the time I was growing up were non-Chinese, many expats never acquired the ability to speak Cantonese. It was expected that Chinese people would communicate with them in English. It was all very colonial.

By the time Mary came to sit her leaving examinations, the older siblings were all out at work and supplementing the family income. David had become an accountant, Eddie an architect and Henry a radio officer in the Merchant Navy, all with a good career prospects in front of them. Mary did not do as well as me, but was allowed to stay on in a private school for years until she was accepted to an art college. Eddie once said to me that this was unfair – I was more suited to continue with education than Mary. However, I was glad Mary got the opportunities that I didn't. At the time I accepted what had happened as simply my lot in life but I think that my experiences of discrimination as a young woman informed my later work on behalf of those who were discriminated against, those who had no voice.

4

Falling in Love

When I was still working at the Hong Kong Telephone Company, at the age of nineteen, I fell in love with Denis, a quantity surveyor. Denis was one of a group of my brother Eddie's colleagues, and socialised with him even after Eddie quit his job as a quantity surveyor to embark on a degree course in architecture at the University of Hong Kong. They were part of a lively group of friends and I would sometimes go with them to the cinema, or swimming in the lukewarm sea in the bays on the southern side of Hong Kong Island and barbecuing afterwards. I liked the camaraderie of these young men. They were full of life and fun.

Tall, handsome and in a 'golden rice-bowl' job – a permanent position in a government department – Denis was an attractive and eligible young man. Mother was pleased and became very fond of him, but Eddie utterly opposed the liaison. He claimed that Denis was mediocre in his work as a surveyor, but his main gripe was that he was using his friendship with Eddie to get near me. I thought this was not only untrue but also unfair. Eddie was more in favour of another of his friends for me, a bright and ambitious surveyor who was keen on me as well. That friend sadly died suddenly from a brain tumour a few years later while still in his late twenties. I presume the thought did not escape Eddie that, had he insisted that I marry his friend, he would have made a young widow of his sister.

Being stubborn, the opposition from Eddie, to whom most of our family listened, drove me further into Denis's arms. In fact, I had fallen head-over-heels in love with him. He was good looking, with a broad forehead, lovely eyes and a beguiling smile, which showed off his perfect teeth. Factoring in a steady, well-paid government job, there was no doubt that he was more than adequate for any twenty-year-old like me – that is, attractive enough but not outstanding in any way. Denis wanted us to get married the following year, but I was not sure if I wanted to be a married woman yet.

My colleagues at the bank were also very friendly and Denis and I would socialise a lot with a few couples in the evenings and at weekends. At one party I met Terence, the husband of a colleague. With an impressive track-record as an account executive, Terence had just left a large advertising company to set up his own agency. A few days later he asked me if I would be interested in becoming his personal assistant. I jumped at the chance. Terence then joined forces with a well-known photographer and an arts director from another advertising firm and this trio of really smart and talented men established a new and dynamic advertising company, LTZ, using the initials of their surnames. The company grew rapidly and, by the time I left when I was twenty-three, they had some sixty staff and I was the trusted PA to the managing director.

When Terence offered me employment it was on condition

that I acquire secretarial skills. Since leaving school I had longed for better qualifications, which would enable me to find a more meaningful career. I had been going to evening classes, studying for O and A levels, and had gone on to learn drawing from an art lecturer. When this opportunity with LTZ arose, I dutifully changed course and started learning shorthand, going up to a speedier class every year. I studied at night for nearly five years until I left Hong Kong in January 1974.

Whilst it was thrilling working in the arts and advertising scene, I saw many indiscretions and infidelities. It was a time of change. The swinging sixties, which had brought sexual freedom and an increasing tendency towards materialism, were having an effect. Eastern morals and sexual codes were starting to seem old-fashioned and out of date. The young wanted to be westernised and liberated.

I blossomed in the new and exciting setting of public relations, working with clients, ambitious artists and young executives. The job opened my eyes to a new world in the commercialised fast lane of Hong Kong. I became more self-confident, outgoing and fashionable in my appearance, with stylish clothes and a trendy hairstyle. I met some young secretaries who bragged about working as temps in London and having a great time sightseeing and meeting new people. I yearned for that kind of adventure.

Denis, my boyfriend, was quite conservative and was uncomfortable with my new look and job environment. He wanted a steady, conventional woman to be his wife, not someone who would drink and smoke in public, for example. It soon became clear that the writing was on the wall.

In the event, my first love affair ended amicably. It would have been a disaster if we had married. Denis was a decent guy, but somewhat lacking in ambition and drive. He was fully content to have a set routine as a civil servant and a steady family life with a biddable wife and children. I would have felt utterly stifled by those conventions, which dictated that a woman should be a dutiful housewife, subservient to her husband. There's no doubt in my mind, though, that my Chinese upbringing meant that I had much lower expectations than a Western woman that marriage would be an equal and fulfilling partnership.

Feeling a bit down, I went on a package holiday to Taiwan on my own in 1972. It was uncommon for a young Hong Kong woman to travel abroad alone in those days, but I was able to afford a foreign holiday for the first time and I was not prepared to hang around looking for a girlfriend willing and able to go with me. It was my first time in an aeroplane and I happened to sit beside a co-pilot from the airline who was also going on holiday to Taiwan. We chatted and he asked for my telephone number. I gave him my card but really did not expect to see him again. In fact, he called the following week when he flew from Singapore to Hong Kong, which was a routine trip for him.

Despite being tanned and well built, Jeff could not have been called handsome. I fell, probably, for his uniform – he looked so smart and had such an air of authority in his crisp white pilot's uniform. We got into a close relationship and I had my first experience of physical intimacy with a man. Premarital sexual relationships were frowned on in the seventies; I know my mother probably guessed what was going on, but she said nothing.

I brought Jeff home once but Mother was not particularly impressed. He could not communicate with her – he only spoke English and Mandarin being an ethnic Chinese from Singapore. Mother definitely preferred Denis to Jeff.

I met other young men, too. My cousin, Wai Chuen, a dental technician, sublet a flat in North Point to two *gweiloes:* a Canadian engineer named Roy and a Belfast journalist named David Watson. When Chinese people first encountered Caucasians – Portuguese or Spanish sailors arriving China in the sixteenth century – it must have been a shock to see them, with their white skin, blue eyes and wavy fair hair. They called them *gweiloes* or 'ghost-men' and the term is now commonly used. It is even included in the *Oxford English Dictionary*. Some regarded the term as derogatory, but many westerners found it endearing. David called himself a *gweilo* proudly. The more polite term is *sai-yan* – 'westerners'.

Roy and David were invited to my cousin's wedding banquet. It was a fine example of the standard nine-course feast for weddings, taking all evening to consume. It was a tradition that delayed many marriages – the young man often had to save for years to pay for this ostentatious meal for hundreds of guests from both the bride's and groom's side. Many couples, alternatively, borrowed the money from relatives or money-lenders and took years to repay it. Parents wanted elaborate weddings for their children – the bigger, the better – but I think people are now more pragmatic in Hong Kong and prefer much smaller events.

Immediately on my arrival at the plush restaurant, lavishly decorated for the occasion in red and gold with the 'double-happiness' banners and symbols for marriage covering the walls, I was taken and planted between the two *gweiloes* at their table. Their interpreter began to explain about each course of rare dishes, such as shark's-fin soup, abalone, white poached chicken and so on. Roy and David had never attended a Chinese wedding before and were naturally fascinated by the delicacies and the ritual ceremony.

Roy was easy to understand, with only a slight Canadian accent, but I found David, with his mixture of Tyrone and Belfast accents, hard to make out. Somehow I gathered that he had arrived just a couple of months before and had not been to any places of interest. I sensed he was lonely, not knowing many people and finding his way around the busy and crowded city, so I gave him a card with my office contact details on it, so that we could get together for a bit of sightseeing. He seemed really pleased, promising to telephone me. Looking back, my invitation probably would have appalled my uncles and aunts – it was not the thing for a respectable young Chinese woman to do. First of all, young females were supposed to be demure and never proactive in dating men, let alone men they had just met. Worse was to invite a foreigner out – there was a great deal of social segregation between *gweiloes* and indigenous Chinese people and I had never been out with one before. The fact was, though, I never regarded it as a date – just a bit of hospitality.

When I did not hear from David for a couple of weeks, I called him. Apparently, he had rung my office but, probably, our receptionist had not been able to understand him and had not passed any message on to me. We met for a drink in an upmarket bar in Central District and David asked me what I would like. The large majority of Chinese people at the time were teetotal and it was taboo for women to drink alcohol in public. Some men would occasionally drink beer on a hot day. I had tried sips of beer at a beach barbecue but had not liked it. I told him I was not familiar with alcohol but would try something not too strong. He ordered me a Pimm's cocktail, which looked very decorative. Before long I was tipsy and I nearly fell off my tall stool at the bar. We joked about it over the years – 'Never give Anna any Pimm's!'

I took him up the Victoria Peak in the Peak Tram, which ascended the hill almost vertically. We marvelled at the spectacular views of the island skyline and the peninsula of Kowloon, taking in the wonderful sights of ocean liners alongside Chinese junks in Victoria Harbour. On another couple of occasions we had dinner with friends of mine. David had just learned to use chopsticks and was very proud of the chance to show off his new skill.

Whilst there were dozens of Chinese newspapers in Hong Kong, there were only two English-language newspapers: the *Standard* and the *South China Morning Post*. The latter had a wider circulation and was well respected in east Asia. David joined the *Standard* first, then went to work for the *Post* as a general news reporter. On one of the occasions when we met, we talked about a particular media story in which a bus conductor had kicked someone off a packed bus in Kowloon. Buses were usually very full during peak traffic hours and bus conductors were among the most hated public-utilities workers in Hong Kong – they decided which passengers were allowed onto the buses and which were not. There was public outrage about the incident and the media was fuelling it. To my surprise, David defended bus conductors, saying that they were badly paid and worked long and unsocial hours inside stiflingly hot buses – we should not be too hard on the offending man, he thought. It was quite a revelation for me that a high-and-mighty *gweilo* could be sympathetic towards a lowly bus conductor.

Nonetheless, like many passengers, he was critical of the fact that the commonly used type of buses in Hong Kong, with small windows and upholstered seats bought from England, were totally unsuitable for our climate. Few people in Hong Kong failed to realise that these purchases were good business for the mother country – and that profit for the British was triumphing over the good of the public. (Wrightbus from Ballymena now supply many air-conditioned modern buses to the millions of residents in Hong Kong.)

Despite his open-neck shirt and jeans, his chain-smoking and his fondness for beer, David impressed me with his liberal views and a perspective that was wider than that of many people in Hong Kong. The fact that he did not associate himself with the usual circle of expats and chose to live in a predominantly Chinese area of North Point rather than in the Mid-Levels was, I later found out, characteristic of him. My cousin's family more or less adopted him and my sixth aunt looked after him when he was ill before he left Hong Kong for good in 1974. I knew that David was interested in me but at that time I felt that the cultural gap was too wide to bridge. Anyway, I was seeing Jeff whenever he was in Hong Kong.

Not long after, Jeff told me he was going to London for training for six months in early 1974, which would raise his chances of promotion to the position of pilot. Since I had heard about other young secretaries' adventures in London I had wanted to go to see a bit of Europe, so I seized on the idea of quitting my job and heading out to London at the same time as him. However, he was lukewarm about the idea of my joining him but that didn't put me off as I had always wanted to go away and have an adventure. It was just convenient that Jeff was going. So that I could get a visa to enter and stay in the UK, I enrolled as a student in a three-month course in a secretarial school in Earls Court, near the hotel in Kensington where Jeff was going to stay. I could see myself working for a while afterwards and hopping off to the continent for a bit, but I had no definite plan of what I might do, nor of the costs involved. All I knew was that I was finding Hong Kong too confined and yearned to spread my wings.

I told my mother I was going to London while Jeff was there. She did not object and my father did not express an opinion either for or against the idea. Fearful of the cold British weather, Mother bought me an exquisite thick quilt in turquoise and made a blue patterned cover for it. I used the quilt during the months I was in London. Later on, my own boys used it, with new covers featuring their favourite film icons. Mother also spent quite a bit of money on a 24-carat gold chain for emergencies – I could sell it if ever I needed money. Thankfully I never needed to cash it in. I keep the chain in memory of her.

5

London: January–October 1974

Seeing people off at the airport was an exciting event for the people of Hong Kong in the early seventies. Before the advent of cheap package holidays, flying was still quite uncommon, and the Kai Tak Airport on the Kowloon Peninsula was on our doorstep. Kai Tak was apparently one of the two most dangerous airports in the world at the time – the other was in Gibraltar. Planes had to fly in between the two mountain ranges on the island and the peninsula, steering over vastly populated towns of tall buildings and landing on a strip of runway that stretched out into the harbour. Those who had the amazing experience of flying into Kai Tak recalled looking right into people's living rooms or seeing washing hung on bamboo poles projecting from balconies.

On 4 January 1974 I had a big send off from my close family and cousins, after an obligatory farewell lunch at the airport restaurant and lots of photographs with me wearing the new wine-coloured jumper lovingly knitted by my mother, and a great big grin on my face. Mother, however, looked grim. I checked my big suitcase, stuffed with my new quilt, some more thick jumpers and thermal underwear (Mother was so worried about the cold weather in the UK, she insisted on long johns), waved everyone goodbye and boarded the plane to London. It was an eighteen-hour flight with two stops for refuelling. As I looked out of the window when we finally approached Heathrow Airport, I was both excited and apprehensive about what lay ahead.

Jeff met me at the airport and took me to my hostel, which was on a list of recommended accommodation from the secretarial college in Earls Court that I had enrolled myself in. It was an international hostel for females on Kensington Road and, by Hong Kong rental standards, the price was surprisingly reasonable. When I got to the Victorian terraced house in the prestigious SW7 district, I realised why. I found myself at the top of several flights of stairs in the attic room, where a member of staff hastily added a single bed for me, right next to the draughty door. I had to share the room with three other young women.

I spent the weekend in Jeff's plush hotel, just around the corner from the hostel, and started my course the following Monday. One morning during that first week, I woke up to lots of excited noises in the hostel and went downstairs to find out what was going on. It had been snowing the night before. This was my first sight of real snow. The other girls, who were mostly foreigners, all gathered inside the opened door and gazed out onto the street, admiring the scene. Innocently, I rushed out onto the pavement and immediately fell flat on my back. Little did I know that snow, as well as being a crisp white, is actually wet and slippery.

It was not only the weather that was different in London. Everything was new and challenging. The hostel food was awful – mostly plain boiled meat and potatoes – and nothing like the tasty

Cantonese cuisine I was accustomed to. But communication was the biggest hurdle. Although I had been taught in school to speak, read and write English, and in fact had been taught through the medium of English at my secondary school, I was used to Chinese teachers and their accent. Here I faced a huge variation of accents, colloquialisms that I had never encountered in my textbooks and the great speed at which local people spoke. I felt quite stupid and excluded at times when I did not understand what people around me were talking about.

I improved a bit after three months in my secretarial course, both in my shorthand speed and my understanding of spoken English, but I still struggled to keep up a conversation in a group of people. In the hostel I got friendly with a young Indian woman who was studying for postgraduate qualifications in medicine and a young Malaysian woman, who introduced me to some of her college friends. I went with them one weekend to the Lake District in a hired minibus driven by one of the guys. It surprised me that they all seemed so confident and not one bit homesick like me.

I saw Jeff mostly at weekends when he was off from training. We would dash off to Chinatown for *dim-sum* lunch and maybe a matinee in the cinema. Unlike me, he was not interested in the arts, but I dragged him to the national galleries to look at the paintings I had so often seen in art books. I stood absolutely mesmerised, in awe of the enormous, centuries-old paintings by world-famous artists.

After a couple of months in the hostel, I moved into a flat in Olympia with four other young women I had met – a couple of

Spanish sisters, Mary from Reading and Jill from the north of England. The sisters were secretaries, Mary worked in the civil service and Jill was a beautician. I shared a room with Mary, who taught me how to peel potatoes with a table knife, as we did not have a potato peeler. She took me home one weekend to her parents' house in Reading, which was really nice of her. It was lovely to get out of London for a couple of days.

When my course finished, I found a temporary secretarial job in a small firm some distance from Olympia and later switched to work more centrally in the London office of a geological-research organisation, which applied for a work permit for me. The people who worked there were mostly geologists coming to London for meetings or conferences and were all very civilised and polite.

At the end of June, Jeff finished his six-month training course and was ready to leave to go back to Singapore. I would have liked to have gone to Singapore with him but, in a difficult conversation, he told me that he had a girlfriend in Singapore as well as me in Hong Kong. What's more, this was a situation he intended to maintain. I was astounded by the revelation and my pride was wounded, but I could not say I was heartbroken. With Jeff around me for six months in London, though, I had not really made as many friends as I might have. I knew I was going to feel a bit lost without him. However, we parted on good terms, without a scene, and promised to see each other in Hong Kong. I never saw him again.

I decided to stay in London. My plan was to work for a little longer, improve my English and save a bit more money for a holiday in Europe, then head home to Hong Kong. But that was not to be.

In early July, soon after Jeff's departure, David Watson, the journalist whom I had met through my cousin, arrived at the door of my flat after a long-distance phone call from Hong Kong. David had left Hong Kong after two years and was looking for a place to stay temporarily while he found a job in London. As the two Spanish sisters had just left, we agreed that he could move in with us for a while. I was shocked to see David looking gaunt and exhausted. Apparently, he had been suffering from stress for a long time. The last straw had been getting a serious threat from a criminal gang he had exposed in his newspaper – he had been nicknamed 'crusader Watson' by the local press. It looked like the hustle and bustle of the mega-city had taken its toll on him.

Compared to Jeff, who was stocky, David was quite tall and thin, full of nervous energy. At twenty-six, he was a lot more worldly than me. He was intelligent, well read and well travelled. He had hitch-hiked around Europe in his teenage years and taken a two-month trek from London to Hong Kong overland. I found him very knowledgeable about current and world affairs, something I was certainly not, having been cocooned in a British colony where there was very little public participation in politics and not much talk about rights and equality. Hong Kong culture, by and large, tended to be materialistic, with a focus on achieving financial success. David's more socialist perspective impressed me. Although he initially seemed to be a stereotypical press hack – chain-smoking, beer-loving, fast-talking – I later realised how sensitive and shy he really was.

The hurt from my breakup with Jeff was still quite raw and, one weekend when no one else was in the flat, I broke down and told David all about it. Somehow we ended up in bed together. David told me he had fallen in love with me the evening we met at my cousin's wedding nearly two years previously. I had known he was interested in me in Hong Kong, but the cultural differences had seemed insurmountable. After living in London for a while, that gap had narrowed. Now we were both strangers in London, lonely, adrift and looking for an anchor.

After searching for a job without success for several weeks, in August David returned to work for the *Belfast Telegraph* in Northern Ireland. We talked on the phone daily. During the August bank holiday I went to Belfast and met his mother, Trudy, and his younger brother, Nicholas, both of whom were warm and welcoming. David's sister, Stephanie, lived in England with her partner. Trudy, looking incredibly young and lively in her mid-forties, was very different from my mother, who tended to be shy when she met strangers. I had a lovely stay, sightseeing along the Antrim coast, enjoying a picnic in the Mourne Mountains – David's favourite spot in Northern Ireland – and visiting a few pubs. Before I left, David asked me to marry him. I responded with an evasive, 'Yes, well, let's see.' It was not really a serious proposal and there was no immediate need for an answer. So it seemed to me that weekend, at any rate. I did not really expect to return to scenic Northern Ireland too soon.

However, in September the Home Office informed the geology organisation that my work-permit application had been rejected.

The Home Office sent me a letter giving me ten days to leave the UK; by the time I received the notification, there were only eight days left. It was brutal. This experience of near-deportation certainly gave me empathy later in my career for those who faced the same and even worse immigration issues.

In horror, I rang David and told him I would be leaving within days. He replied, 'Don't worry – let's get married!' Within twenty-four hours, he got an MP to contact the Home Office and I got my visa extended for a month so that we could marry. I was hesitant about it and wanted to return home, but he was very persuasive. We both knew that, if I left, the relationship would end – and neither of us wanted that. I relented and got swept away by the excitement of getting married and going to live in Northern Ireland.

However, my flatmate Mary and the geologists were aghast that I was choosing to move to the most troubled spot in the UK. It was October 1974, just a few months after the Ulster Workers' Council strike, which had seen two weeks of road blocks, intimidation and violence, and had brought down the first power-sharing Northern Ireland Assembly and Executive. The chaos had been reported widely by all the mainstream press and television channels in the UK.

Mary was the only real friend I had in London and, being very down to earth, she was also concerned that I had agreed to marry David so soon after breaking up with Jeff. Looking back, if it had not been for the predicament I was in regarding my immigration status, the whirlwind romance might just have fizzled out over a few months and I might have returned to Hong Kong. I told

Mary I had genuinely fallen in love with David and liked what I had seen in Northern Ireland during the August weekend. I was prepared to give it a go. After all, there were over a million people living there, leading normal lives. And we could always return to London or Hong Kong if it was really bad.

Knowing my severe lack of culinary skills, Mary wisely gave me a great big cookery book as a wedding gift – which I still use occasionally even now.

6

First Impressions of Northern Ireland

I quit my job with the geologists and flew to Northern Ireland at the end of September, not without some doubt in my mind as to whether I was doing the right thing in marrying David. I did feel some trepidation, too, about Northern Ireland itself, given the continued unrest; but David had agreed that if I did not like it we could move back to London. He was vague, however, about living in Hong Kong again. I promised I would give it a go for six months – and here I am, still in Northern Ireland over forty years later.

When I told my mother about getting married to David, she was understandably less than overjoyed, but not for the reasons I expected. I thought she might oppose it on the grounds of safety, or mixed marriage. Her eldest sister had been vehemently opposed to her daughter, my cousin, wanting to marry an Australian she had met at university in London. Mother's reservations, however, were more pragmatic. She was concerned about David's health, knowing that he had been unwell prior to leaving the colony, and about how far away I would be if I settled in Northern Ireland. I tried my best to reassure her. I could see that David was getting better and I promised her that I would visit her or that she could come to see us in Northern Ireland.

David and I got married on 7 October 1974 in the Belfast Registry Office. I wore a long red velvet skirt with a gold blouse, which were the traditional colours for Chinese weddings. Although not exactly the traditional red Chinese wedding costume, elaborately embroidered in gold and silver thread and depicting the meeting of a dragon and a phoenix as a symbol of marital harmony, I was satisfied. At least the colours reflected the spirit of a Chinese wedding. I was a bit disappointed that my father could not attend the wedding because of another bout of lung problems, a legacy of the tuberculosis he had contracted during the war, but I was pleased that my second-eldest brother, Eddie, was able to come to represent my family.

With David and I both being broke and with the haste of the wedding, it had to be a simple affair. Back home, getting married would take months, if not years, of saving up and organisation, culminating in a lavish buffet dinner like the one at which David and I had met. Thankfully, I was always quite practical and matter of fact, so I was content for the wedding to be uncomplicated. David's brother, Nicholas, commented to his mother that few women in Northern Ireland would contemplate marrying without an engagement ring on their finger.

'Well,' I said, 'that's not a Chinese custom!'

We did not have money for a hotel reception or a honeymoon, let alone a diamond ring, but it was true that Chinese people did not always go for a formal engagement announcement and a ring to mark the period before a wedding – not in the seventies, anyway. We did get a long weekend in Dublin a few weeks later and I bought a small sapphire and diamond ring in Belfast.

On the evening of the wedding, we had a wonderful buffet dinner in my mother-in-law's house, with a beautiful spread of cooked meat, salads and mouthwatering desserts prepared by David's cousin Mark Hegan, who was a professional chef. I changed from my red-and-gold outfit into a traditional Chinese evening dress, a *cheongsam*, with a high collar and side splits, which I had brought over from Hong Kong. Never having been to any wedding in the UK, I had no notion beforehand that it is a tradition for guests to kiss the bride. Kissing is a particularly western way of expressing affection – it does not happen in Chinese culture, especially not in public or between strangers. In fact, decorum dictates that a bride should look shy and demure. I had never been kissed by so many people in my life until the evening of the reception. This was certainly my induction into western society.

My mother-in-law, Trudy, and I got on like a house on fire. Following her husband's untimely death from a brain tumour, she returned in her early forties to full-time education. She had graduated from Queen's University that summer and become a lecturer in French and communications in Rupert Stanley College. David was full of admiration for his mother. Nicholas, a super-bright teenager, was still at Methodist College and we became very fond of each other. David and I moved into a converted flat in a red-brick Victorian house on Cyprus Avenue in east Belfast, near Trudy, who had lived in that area for many years. Incidentally, the house sat next to the home of the founder and leader of the Democratic Unionist Party (DUP), the Reverend Ian Paisley.

Little did I know then how many times I would cross paths and swords with 'the big man' of Northern Irish politics. I also learned from Nicholas that a world-famous singer-songwriter called Van Morrison had written a song about Cyprus Avenue. The song was such a part of Morrison's repertoire that, in 2015, the renowned singer held an open-air concert at the end of the street, attracting hundreds of fans. The event, taking place against the beautiful backdrop of the green, leafy avenue, was broadcast to millions across the world.

We saw a lot of Trudy, Nicholas and David's granny, who lived with her eldest daughter, Maureen Tattersall, and her two daughters, nearby. They were all very welcoming and I was instantly made to feel part of the extended family.

As soon as the wedding was over, I applied for a job as the secretary to the editor of *Farmweek*, a local agricultural newspaper. To my great surprise I got the position after an interview, despite my lack of fluency in English and total ignorance of farming and country life. The editor, Hal Crowe, was a gentleman who was well respected by the staff and the paper's readers. When he dictated to me his weekly editorial, all of its farming and policy terminology was like another language to me. The draft editorials I typed up often needed corrections – all of which he tolerated with great patience and kindness. At the end of my first day he said, 'See you in the morning,' to which I replied, 'Which morning'? I had so much to learn.

There were many other staff members in the office working in reporting, photography and administration. They were really a lovely bunch of colleagues and I got friendly with a number of young women, one of whom was Vivien, who worked in advertising. One afternoon, Vivien took me in her car to the office of our printer in Lurgan. We drove down the Lisburn Road to get to the motorway, but there was traffic congestion, with cars bumper to bumper all the way. We found ourselves stuck behind an army vehicle with its door wide open and a very young-looking soldier sitting next to the open door, with his rifle pointing outwards. Every time there was a sudden noise, he jumped nervously and held the weapon up as if he was about to fire. After a while, I got a stomach ache from the tension of being so close to such an edgy military man. I said this to Vivien, who tried to leave as big a gap as possible between us and the armoured truck. Luckily it turned down a side street soon afterwards. I was grateful for her understanding and for not dismissing me as a silly little foreigner.

I liked the quietness of the city of Belfast. There were fewer people, less traffic and less noise than in the day-and-night hustle and bustle of Hong Kong and London. I did not see many restaurants about, though, and asked Vivien where she dined out. She replied that Belfast people did not go out to restaurants any more – many of them had been closed or bombed out. She said that she and her husband only went out to dinner for wedding anniversaries or birthdays. It was a shock to me, as I was used to eating out in Hong Kong and London – never in particularly expensive restaurants, of course, but the large range of eateries meant that there was plenty of opportunity to eat inexpensively.

I noticed, too, that many cinemas had their shutters down. Nicholas knew I loved the arts and, one evening, took me to the

Arts Theatre on Botanic Avenue, which seemed to be one of the few entertainment venues left in Belfast. Sadly, that closed too a few years later.

Belfast city centre was surrounded by a ring of steel, with entry and exit points manned by security staff who carried out body searches and checked handbags and belongings. I thought, given the circumstances, that it was a reasonable preventative measure, but I nevertheless found it frustrating to have my bag searched every time I went into a shop. Granted, at times the searches were pretty perfunctory, but people going from shop to shop were searched incessantly.

It was eerie to observe office workers and shoppers all hurrying out of the city centre by 7 or 8 o'clock in the evening, leaving behind a deserted city centre, like a ghost town, after dark. It was a stark contrast to the thriving night-time economy of Hong Kong and London, where the streets were thronged with people and the shops and restaurants were all lit up with multicoloured neon lights. I did miss the nightlife that I had been so used to in the two cosmopolitan cities.

I did not tell my mother about any of these problems; instead I told her how friendly people were. I found it very curious when I got onto the bus every morning that many passengers would be chatting to each other. The bus would always be buzzing with the noise of people talking. I thought they must all know each other somehow, until one morning a total stranger started a conversation with me. It dawned on me that people talked to strangers in Belfast – unlike in other big cities, where they were always guarded.

One afternoon, I was on a bus with a colleague on my way home. There was a bomb alert, which brought traffic to a standstill for hours. I was glad that the colleague was on the bus as I would not have known what to do or how to get home on foot. She and a number of other female passengers decided to go to the Skandia, probably the only restaurant open in the city centre at the time, and invited me along. They told me they had all got to know each other just by taking the same bus to and from work most days. This seemed incredible to me, as someone who had lived her life up to then in cities where people were suspicious of strangers because of the high crime rate. When my colleague told them I had just got married, they treated me to dinner, which was really touching, as they had only just met me.

David introduced me to some of his friends and colleagues, who were all very friendly. I met the columnist Billy Simpson in McGlade's Bar, a pub near the *Belfast Telegraph*'s offices that many journalists frequented at lunchtime and after work. Billy was very funny, firing joke after joke in rapid succession and causing his colleagues to fall about laughing, but I could not understand his humour at all. I found the occasion utterly embarrassing. It was humiliating to gawk at them without being able to follow the flow of in-jokes about people and politicians. Although I knew that no one was trying to exclude me, I felt left out and lonely. Nonetheless, Billy and his wife, Daphne, became good friends of ours and I gradually came to enjoy his humour as I became immersed in Northern Irish life.

In the postwar boom years the British government relaxed immigration restrictions to allow people from many

Commonwealth countries to come to the UK to help meet the labour shortage. However, with the Troubles raging on, not many black or minority-ethnic people came to live in Northern Ireland. It was rare to see non-white people on the streets of Belfast. On several occasions I found people staring at me – generally, I thought, out of curiosity rather than hostility.

On another afternoon in McGlade's, I was introduced to Gerry Fitt, a politician from the Social Democratic and Labour Party (SDLP). I sat beside him amongst several other journalists and, every time I looked around at him, I could see that he was staring at me. I felt a bit unnerved. After we left the pub, I could not help expressing some dismay to David that this middle-aged friend of his had been looking at me the whole time. Was it because I was Chinese? Shaking his head and giving a great belly laugh, David enlightened me – Gerry had some difficulties with his sight that meant he appeared to be looking sideways. The eye that I thought was staring at me was in fact not seeing much of anything at all.

David's friends were friendly and hospitable, although I was a bit puzzled about why they wanted to befriend me as they must have had plenty of friends and family. I think that notion came from being brought up in a British colony where Caucasians did not mix much with indigenous Chinese people. That segregation somehow instilled a sense in us that white people were aloof and regarded themselves as superior. It was really internalised racism that I was experiencing at the time, believing, almost, that I was unworthy of people's interest and attention.

As well as basking in the kindness and friendliness of its people, I discovered Northern Ireland's wonderful countryside.

David was a keen hiker and used to enjoy youth-hostelling around Ireland, although some of the youth hostels in the north were closed because of the Troubles. I kitted myself out with new walking boots, a rucksack and outdoor clothing, ready for action. I fell in love with the Mourne Mountains, the Antrim coast, the forest parks, Lough Erne and many other scenic places. We spent most weekends hiking, staying in cheap hostels or bed-and-breakfast accommodation. I conquered Slieve Donard with a storm of hailstones beating down on us, although my legs suffered for several days afterwards.

It was fortunate that I found something enjoyable to do at weekends. Most young women in Hong Kong were fashion conscious and would spend their weekends shopping. I was no different until I got to the shops in Belfast. At only 5 feet and ¾ inches in height and a mere 6.5 stone in weight, with a dress size of 6 and a shoe size of 3, it was almost impossible for me to find clothes or shoes that would fit in Northern Ireland, where the average height for women was 5 inches taller and the average shape 4 dress sizes bigger. On a few occasions, when I had to buy a new outfit or an evening dress, I ended up going home empty-handed after hours of searching vainly from shop to shop. After a while, I just gave up shopping to avoid disappointment and had my sister send me clothes now and then. There was no petite range in any shops in the seventies. Thank goodness, there is plenty of choice now, but I mostly just shop online these days – sadly, no longer for a size 6.

Another fashionable pursuit for Chinese women in Hong Kong was to get a stylish perm for their straight, black hair, in order to provide a bit of wave and body. I had quite long hair in London and decided now to have it cut to shoulder length and get a slight perm. I went to a hairdresser on the Upper Newtownards Road, near our flat, and told her what I wanted – just a slight wave at the end of the hair. Unfortunately, she had never handled strong, straight, voluminous Chinese hair before. After the chemical failed to have any effect the first time, she applied it again. I came out of the salon with a head of frizzy, curly hair – not what I wanted at all.

When I went back to the office on Monday, Vivien screamed at me, 'What have you done to your beautiful hair? It's absolutely ruined!' She gave me the name of a very good hairdresser in the city centre and I had it all cut off into a short hairstyle. It was quite smart, really, and the *Farmweek* photographer took a photograph of me smiling when I returned the next day to the office.

Abandoning shopping and perms were not difficult tasks, though, compared to the other adjustments I had to make. So many things were alien to me – the culture, the systems, the climate, the geography, the diet and the language. One day, shortly after we moved into the flat, David asked me to let the milkman know about a change in delivery. I looked at him blankly – I had no idea how to contact the milkman or even how to address one in written form. I had never had a milkman before, ever. Should I write, 'Dear Mr Milkman …'? Even very simple acts could be a mystery in a strange country. At times I felt that I had been reduced from a grown adult, self-confident and self-assured, to a child, who always had to seek guidance in new situations.

Even though I had managed to improve my fluency in London,

English was still my second language and the speed at which people talked as well as their many different accents really baffled me. The only person I could totally understand was Trudy, who pronounced her words precisely, because of her background in teaching French and communication. In the first few months of our marriage at least, I missed half of what David said, and David could only say a few words in Cantonese.

I love Chinese food and craved proper Cantonese cuisine. There was a Chinese restaurant in Belfast city centre and a few takeaways in east Belfast, but they did not, to me, offer authentic Chinese cooking. I dreamt about eating Cantonese roast duck, *char-siu* (barbecue pork) and steamed dumplings. I regretted the fact that I had never learned to cook at home. Mother and Grandmother had never wanted anyone to get in their way when they were cooking. I had been too busy working and socialising, anyway, to have the desire to learn.

Mother sent me some cookery books and I gradually learned to prepare some dishes. However, David was not particularly keen on having Chinese food with rice every day, so we tended often to have straightforward western-style food with potatoes – which, to Chinese people, are just a type of vegetable used occasionally to complement a beef or lamb stew. There is a joke among Hong Kong people that, if you live in the UK, you have to 'suffer' the diet of potatoes. However, we compromised by having Chinese food at weekends, when Trudy usually came for dinner.

Practicalities aside, I realised after a while that people's feelings are very much the same, no matter what country they come from. Love, hatred, joy, anger, envy and compassion are identical all over the world, but how people express or suppress these feelings varies greatly between eastern and western cultures. Frequently in those early days I struggled with internal conflict about the extent to which I should shake off my inherited culture and identity as a Chinese woman in order to fit into Northern Irish society. I did not want to seem odd or peculiar to local people, who mostly seemed to welcome me with open arms, but I was conscious that I often thought and behaved differently from others in my adoptive country.

The philosophy of Confucius has, by and large, influenced Chinese thinking for two thousand years and its emphasis on achieving harmony – and conformity – has shaped the values and behaviour of many Chinese people for centuries. The patriarchal culture requires women to be subservient to their male relations. To a large extent, I could see that reflected in my mother's life. Collective thinking and action for the common good are valued by Chinese families, while individualism can be seen as selfish and deviant. It is not uncommon for Chinese families to have three generations living together under the same roof, having to compromise and sacrifice their individual needs and desires in order to keep harmony and peace within the family unit. David's desire to be independent and individualistic was at odds with the culture in which I had grown up, and it took me a while to understand it. The fact that he wanted his own space at times was not intended to be a rejection.

Very often, Chinese people appear to westerners to be reserved, polite and passive, while many Chinese people find westerners loud, direct and pushy. Despite a few occasions when

I felt uncomfortable with (in my view) blunt comments, I soon appreciated the directness and straight-talking of people here. And I was always mindful of balancing my instinct for being courteous with the need not to come across to local people as insincere. There was so much to learn about the subtle cultural differences between the places David and I came from. Even fairly recently, I mentioned to someone who knows me well in Northern Ireland that I am very much westernised now. He replied that I am perhaps more Chinese than I think.

7

Settling Down

One Sunday afternoon, about a year after I came to live in Belfast, while I was washing my hands and looking into the mirror in our bathroom, I suddenly had a sense of foreboding – something I had never experienced before and never have since. It was what some may call a premonition. I told David about the peculiar sensation and wondered if something bad had happened at home in Hong Kong. David reassured me that I would hear if something was not right.

Two weeks later, on the morning of Saturday, 5 July 1975, when we were getting ready to go out walking with a *Farmweek* colleague and her husband, I found an envelope under our front door that contained a telegram. It came from Eddie, my brother, who said that our father had died on Thursday past but that there was no need to come back for the funeral the following week.

Holding on to the telegram, I felt numb. My friends arrived at that moment. They probably thought I was heartless as I was not showing much emotion, but the news had not sunk in – it was only words on a piece of paper. We cancelled the day out and I telephoned home.

I recall that everyone sounded quite calm. Mother spoke quietly and steadily, but I could hear her voice breaking now and again: 'Your father's lungs progressively deteriorated in the last few months. It was upsetting to watch him breathe with increasing difficulty. He was admitted to hospital a week or so ago and died from lung failure, a consequence of tuberculosis, which damaged parts of his lungs decades ago. It is a relief to us that he won't suffer any longer.' He was only sixty-seven and they had been married for thirty-seven years. I did not go back for the funeral.

It was difficult to explain to myself, never mind to others, why I was not stricken with grief at the loss. My father had always been remote and I had always believed that he did not really care about me, but he was still my father and it should have been a deep bereavement. I think it was because I had not seen him fall ill and it just seemed so unreal. Also, I had not seen him for a long time and was used to not seeing him, so I did not feel a sense of physical separation from him when he died. It was only five years later, when I went back to Hong Kong and stood in front of his grave, that I finally came to the deep and painful realisation that I would never see him again.

A few months before my father's death, my brother Henry, who is eighteen months older than me, returned to work in Hong Kong after being a ship's radio officer for three years. Henry had qualified as a radio officer in Hong Kong Technical College but had always hoped to go to university overseas, given the fierce competition for entry into the University of Hong Kong. The three years at sea had enabled him to save enough money to support himself for a few years while studying. After a telephone conversation with him, I contacted a Chinese friend, a lecturer at Queen's University, Belfast, to ask if it was possible for him to get a place there. Henry applied to Queen's and was accepted to start a degree in electrical and electronic engineering that September. It was comforting to know that Father had been very pleased that Henry was coming to Belfast to attend university and be with us.

Henry arrived soon after my father's death which was a real comfort to me. Rather than moving into our tiny flat, Trudy kindly said that Henry could live with her in her house, as Nicholas had gone to university in England. We were grateful for her generosity, given that we were still newlyweds and the so-called spare room in the flat was so small that you could hardly swing a cat in it. It was totally out of the question for me to let Henry live in a flat with other students in the university area, the Holylands, paying rent and bills. He was family. Henry filled me in about Father's health towards the end of his life in July and about the funeral, which had been well attended by members of the family from both sides.

It was during that year, too, when David was out one evening, that I heard a loud bang outside. Someone had thrown a petrol bomb at a house opposite our flat, but the car parked on the drive had taken the full force and burst into flames, its windows shattering. Realising instantly that some sort of an explosion had taken place nearby and fearing more to come, I dived behind a sofa until I heard the arrival of the fire brigade and police vehicles. It was a Catholic family who lived in that house. That was my first real glimpse of the nasty sectarian conflict in Northern Ireland.

We all settled into our routines – Henry at Queen's and David and myself going about our daily lives. After a couple of years in the flat, we bought a three-storey terraced house in Oakland Avenue, off the Upper Newtownards Road in east Belfast. Henry moved with us, having the top floor to himself. Henry also worked on holidays and weekends at White Satin, the best-known Chinese restaurant at the time, in Greyabbey, about fifteen miles east of Belfast, riding there and back on his moped.

After working at *Farmweek* for two years, in 1976 I went to work for the BBC in Northern Ireland – first in the personnel department, and then with the World Service. The producer, Virginia Hardy, known as Auntie Gin, was well respected in the corporation and I was very fortunate to have had the opportunity to be trained by her as a production secretary. Gin had lived in Hong Kong – in fact, in the year I was born, 1950, when her brother had been a radio producer in the colony – after which she had gone to work as a secretary in the United Nations in New York. Her brother's second wife was an American-Chinese academic in the USA. He, unfortunately, died in a car accident, when still relatively young. Gin and I clicked right away and we remained in contact for many years after we both left the BBC.

Northern Ireland's input to the World Service was mainly a weekly news commentary slot and regular features on Irish culture. BBC NI also produced Radio 4's *Woman's Hour* four times a year, when that programme was broadcast from Northern Ireland. In addition, we made several different series in music and literature. We had Gloria Hunniford talking to invited guests and playing records, Tommy Sands playing his own music and many other well-known Irish singer-songwriters such as Christy Moore were featured. There were interviews with Irish writers on their published works: most memorable for me were Jennifer Johnston, Dervla Murphy and William Trevor. Before we met Jennifer, Gin brought in a pile of her books and I devoured them. David was envious that I got to meet Dervla Murphy, whose book, *Full Tilt*, had inspired him to travel from Belfast overland to Hong Kong in 1972. Gin produced some excellent programmes on Irish playwrights, such as Brian Friel and Sean O'Casey, as well and I developed a lifelong devotion to their work.

During my time at the BBC I met a number of politicians. I remember collecting the Reverend Ian Paisley from reception and bringing him to the recording studio. In the lift he told me he was having great success with his recent dieting, flapping his jacket to demonstrate how loose it had become. Being aware of his trademark firebrand style, I was quite taken aback by his friendly, affable manner towards me. I was, after all, just a young secretary among many in Broadcasting House.

And, of course, I worked with many well-known presenters and reporters too. Barry Cowan, who sadly passed away some years ago, was a regular contributor, as were Wendy Austin and Seamus McKee, who are still presenting programmes today. The *Spotlight* programme office was just down the corridor from our office and a couple of now-national presenters, Jeremy Paxman and Gavin Esler, worked there for short stints, reporting on the Troubles. Knowing all these journalists was no doubt an advantage in later years when I became a spokesperson for the Chinese community and, of course, after I was elected as a member of the Assembly. Because the setting was familiar to me, I was generally fairly relaxed going to recording studios to be interviewed.

I was also seconded to help with the production of a half-hour television programme about the Chinese community in Northern Ireland, to be presented by Helen Madden. It centred on a young Chinese man, whom I persuaded to take part and looked at different aspects of the Chinese community. After all the filming was done, Helen wrote the narration, part of which I was unhappy with. I felt responsible for showing Chinese people in a sympathetic light after getting them to take part in the programme and I did not want them to feel betrayed. I was probably a bit too sensitive, wanting to protect them as best I could. Eventually some sentences were changed to all our satisfaction and the televised programme was well received by the Chinese community.

A few years later, after I left the BBC, their education department contracted me to present a television programme for schoolchildren about the Chinese community. The short film was widely shown in schools and a special viewing was held at the Chinese-new-year dinner in the Europa Hotel for the Chinese community and invited VIPs. We were pleased that the media were finally focusing on an ethnic-minority community whose existence had been largely disregarded by public authorities.

An offshoot of working in the World Service was that I became a 'stringer' for the BBC's Chinese External Services, which broadcast out of Bush House in London. When they realised that there was a Cantonese native speaker working at BBC Northern Ireland, they snapped me up as a freelance broadcaster who would portray the local lives of the Chinese community and at times report on issues in the wider community. After learning to use the recording equipment, I got out and about, interviewing Chinese chefs, students, academics and medical doctors, probing into their life stories and finding out how and why they had ended up in this far-flung corner of Europe. I made a few short features, too, on the Vietnamese-Chinese community settling into Craigavon and the Women for Peace campaign, interviewing Mairéad Corrigan and Betty Williams.

The good thing was that my mother could listen to my voice over the short-wave radio, broadcast all the way to Hong Kong. However, it was a bit of a challenge for the sound engineers who had to do the editing in the studio when they could not understand a word of the interviews. They always got them right, though, and worked with great professionalism.

Through all these initial contacts with the Chinese community, I realised the hardship and the isolation of Chinese people living in Northern Ireland, many of whom came from the poor rural area of Hong Kong, the New Territories, between mainland China and the Kowloon Peninsula. For many years, there was no compulsory education beyond primary school in Hong Kong and English was not widely taught in primary schools or rural village schools, so many young people did not get the chance to learn much English before emigrating.

On hearing the communication problems Chinese people faced due to their lack of English, my mother-in-law, Trudy, a further-education lecturer, suggested that I set up an evening English class for Chinese residents of Northern Ireland at Rupert Stanley College, where she taught modern languages. We started the first-ever English class for Chinese people in Northern Ireland in 1978 with about twelve students, mostly young men and women who had immigrated into the region.

Although learning English was the aim of the class, it quickly became a social hub. I soon realised that many of our students never ventured out of their shops or homes, which were usually near their place of work. David and I organised trips out on Sundays, leading convoys of cars to the Giant's Causeway, the Antrim coast or south Down. On one occasion we took the students horse riding in Castlewellan Forest Park. Some of them just fell in love with it and organised their own riding activities many times afterwards. They all marvelled at the wonderful spectacle of the volcanic rock formation at the Giant's Causeway. The Giant's Causeway, of course, is now essential viewing for any member of the Chinese community coming to 'Norn Iron'.

I am still in touch with some of the students from the class. Danny Wong, one of the brightest among them, is now a prominent businessman and chair of the Chinese Chamber of Commerce and the Chinese Welfare Association (CWA). Some are founders and active members of the Oi Kwan Women's Group, set up with the help of the Barnardo's Chinese Health Project, for which I became a project worker in later years. Just a couple of months ago I was having *dim-sum* lunch with Corinna Tattersall, David's cousin, and her civil partner, Angie Redmond, when a woman at the next table came over to speak to me. She was one of the students from our 1978 class. Amazingly, we both recognised each other after nearly forty years. When we asked for the bill we realised that she had paid for our lunch. It was a lovely gesture and Corinna and Angie were mightily impressed.

It was in the summer of 1978 that I made my first visit home to Hong Kong after four and a half years away. David and I thought that, after Henry left in a year's time, we should start a family. It seemed a good idea for me to go to Hong Kong before that happened. The three weeks there flew by. I caught up with family and friends as well as enjoying the much-missed authentic Cantonese food.

I stayed in our old three-bedroom flat with Mother, Mary, who was still a student, Eddie and his wife, Lisa, a very able and attractive Eurasian. Eddie and Lisa had moved back home to save on rent and overheads as he had just set up his own architectural firm. With only a meagre civil-servant's pension from my father, Mother depended on Eddie and David for her and Mary's upkeep. David, an accountant, and his wife, Lulu, a health visitor, lived with their toddler son, Raymond, in their own flat in Wan Chai, which was not too far from Mother's home in North Point.

My family was pleased that I had settled well in Northern Ireland, but soon they expressed concerns about the ongoing civil unrest there, which often made world headlines and caused them to worry about our safety. Understandably, they tried to persuade me to come back with David to live in Hong Kong, which was then booming, with unprecedented economic growth and improved public-service provision. They could see lots of opportunities for us both. I promised I would talk to David and we would give it our serious consideration.

I returned to our home in Belfast, excited about the economic progress in Hong Kong and hopeful that we might leave troubled Ulster to live there. However, David was not keen on the idea, not wanting to risk living in that hectic environment again, since it had once caused him great stress. I was deeply disappointed and not without some resentment that he refused to consider the prospect that, being totally bilingual, I would now do well in the British colony. But he insisted, saying, 'As the main breadwinner, it is important for me to stay put in the place I am accustomed to.' I resigned myself to the idea that we would remain in Northern Ireland for the rest of our lives.

Henry graduated from Queen's University in 1979 and got an electronic-engineering job in the General Electric Company in Coventry, which later changed its name to Marconi and thrived until the mid-2000s, when it collapsed. While we were happy that he had found employment so swiftly, I was sad to see him go.

We continued to live for another while in the terraced house on Oakland Avenue, which was cheap to buy and all we could afford without any savings. However, with the help of a Housing Executive grant, we updated it and were able to sell it at a small profit and purchase our second home, a semi-detached house in Holland Gardens, not far away. David earned a lot more than me as a journalist but he never disclosed his salary to me and always had his own bank account. We never had a savings account together either. Perhaps it was the norm for the time, but never having a joint bank account meant that I had to rely on him to manage our money, particularly after I left work and had no income of my own. He would hand me a cheque each month for groceries. Although I never protested, perhaps out of pride, it bothered me that I never knew much about our finances and that he had total control of them.

In 1980, Cathay Pacific established its first flight from Hong Kong to London and Mother and Mary took advantage of a special offer of reduced fares and came to visit us that August. It was a very short visit – only about twelve days, as Mary had to be back for her A-level exam results – but we managed to take them to all the major tourist attractions. It was lovely for them to see where we lived and to enjoy the unspoiled, beautiful countryside. Despite the language barrier, Mother and Trudy were pleased to meet each other.

Meanwhile, the plan for a family was not going as well as we had hoped. Coming off the pill when I was nearly twenty-eight, it took me nine months to start menstruating again. Although we were keen to have a child, we knew we had to be patient. Wanting something to lift my spirits and to cultivate my love for art, I enrolled to do an O-level course in art at night at Rupert Stanley. I thrived in it, and my good results spurred me on to enrol in an A-level night class the following year.

After three frustrating years of trying for a family, the consultant told me to put the idea out of my mind and to be relaxed about it. 'If it happens, it happens,' he said. I decided to quit my secretarial job, which seemed such a dead end, and enrolled in a full-time foundation course for a fine-art degree. Knowing I was feeling low, David supported me as I embarked on this new venture – a long-held ambition. But it didn't happen. David and I went to Hong Kong for a holiday in July 1981, a few months before I was due to begin the course. He returned home after two weeks and I stayed on for a bit longer. In August I discovered, to my surprise and delight, that I was pregnant. We were all elated and I could not wait to get back to Belfast.

I did not want to abandon the art course and started attending classes in September with the other students, nearly all of whom were aged eighteen, fresh from school. I loved it. My strength was in painting portraits of people, a hobby that I had had since childhood. Some of the paintings that I did in those few months still hang on my walls. I dropped out of the course when Conall, our son, was born the following spring. It was a long labour and eventually I had an emergency Caesarean section, but when he was handed to me I knew it had all been worthwhile. Conall, with lots of dark hair and large dark eyes, was a gorgeous baby. We were proud and adoring parents, over the moon with our long-awaited son.

After my initial few months in London, my homesickness had faded away. However, when I returned home from hospital with Conall, I yearned for my mother to be with me. There was a neighbour, a bit younger than me, across the road from our house who had a baby just a couple of weeks after me. I watched her parents arrive before she was discharged from hospital with food and flowers to prepare for her return, and both sets of grandparents were in and out of the house for weeks to give her support. I was green with envy. David did take a week's leave to help out but Trudy was too busy at work and with her packed social schedule to do much. Henry came over from Coventry to see his nephew and took some lovely photographs of the baby, smiling at the camera in his pram beside the window with the sunlight on his face. The doting uncle was pleased as Punch.

We found out that our first-born was very bright, too, very

early on. Being a first-time mum, I bought childcare guru Penelope Leach's seminal book on child development, which became my bible for rearing my two children. It recommended talking to your baby as early and as much as you can. I got into a habit of saying 'What a good boy!' after I changed Conall's nappy and, when he was about six weeks old, he started to repeat the phrase after me, getting better and better at it each time. I did not tell anyone at first; then, one day, when he was lying on the end of the bed reading his newspaper, David heard him and nearly fell off the bed in surprise.

Then our wonderful health visitor, Miss Ballentine, explained that it was not in fact a miracle that Conall could talk at the age of six weeks. In fact, babies try to imitate speech from birth and develop proper and full speech as they grow older. Conall was certainly an early developer, though – he could walk before he was one and talk before he was two.

Miss Ballentine was extremely attentive, knowing that I had no family support around me, and visited us regularly. She recommended that I attend a mother-and-toddler group run by a local church and Conall and I went every week to meet other toddlers and mums. I also got friendly with three women, Heather, Karen and Lynda, whom I had met at the hospital antenatal class. After the birth of the babies we kept in regular contact, visiting each other's homes in turn. Little did we know that Heather and I would one day become in-laws.

After waiting so long to have a baby, I devoted all my time to caring for Conall, playing with him, talking with him and reading to him. He was well stimulated and could read, count and tell the time before he started school without us ever formally teaching him. He went on to be one of the top pupils in his class throughout his schooling.

When Conall was about two years of age, I met a senior police officer at a dinner party, who complimented me on my good command of English and suggested that I should become a police interpreter as there was a great shortage of people with such skills. A week later, I received a telephone call from another police officer, asking me to attend a police station to do some interpreting. I declined the invitation, saying that I had not been recruited formally, never mind properly trained. A few minutes later, a policewoman from the so-called Aliens Department of the Royal Ulster Constabulary (RUC) called, quite puzzled as to why I had declined to attend a session. She reasoned: 'Anna, you speak good English and you're a native Chinese speaker. You'll naturally be able to interpret for your fellow countrymen and women.' That was how I got to become a sessional police interpreter. Needless to say, there are much more stringent recruitment and training procedures now for interpreting for the police, the courts and the health services.

The work, although sporadic, was well paid and quite flexible, which meant that I could go to help with taking statements in the evenings when David was home from work. If I was needed during the day for a court appearance, I would leave Conall with a childminder, Linda, just up the road from our house. We were extremely lucky to have Linda, who was most dependable. She was our childminder for years, until the boys finished primary school.

Chinese people are exceptionally law abiding and hardly ever commit crimes in the UK as a whole. The interpreting was mostly about car accidents, burglaries of Chinese residents' homes or racist damage to business premises. One harrowing case was when a young Chinese woman made an allegation of rape late one night. I had to help with the medical examination and with writing up her statement on the attack, although the case never went to court. Another case concerned a woman arrested and charged for shoplifting when, carrying goods from a department store, she went after her young daughter, who had wandered out of the store onto the street. I believed her from the start and did my best to help her. Apart from feeling I was doing something worthwhile, the money I earned from interpreting came in handy when I was a full-time mum at home and no longer had a salary.

I very much wanted another child and in April 1985 our second son, Owen, was born, a day after Conall turned three. Owen was four weeks early. His brother's big birthday party the day before has often been blamed for his precipitated arrival, but being premature did not do him any harm, even though he was a much smaller baby than Conall. Owen looked more Chinese than Conall, with finer bones and features; while Conall hardly ever slept through the night until he was two years of age, Owen was a most placid baby. Conall absolutely doted on his younger brother as soon as he set eyes on him and came back to visit us in the hospital the next day with a pile of drawings of Owen with a big mop of black hair on top of his head and matchstick arms and legs. The two of them loved and appreciated each other from day one and remain very close now. As it turned out, Owen was just as bright as his big brother, achieving excellent academic results. He was very popular in school, hailed by teachers as a model pupil and well liked by his peers.

Although I enjoyed two healthy pregnancies, for some strange reason I developed an allergy in my nose when I was pregnant with Owen and started to snore badly. David already depended on sleeping pills to get to sleep every night and my snoring exacerbated the problem. We struggled with it and, after Owen's birth, I had an operation to widen my nasal passage and started also using a nasal spray to help me breathe at night. David tried earplugs but did not like them and eventually gave up. He was getting desperate because of lack of sleep, between my snoring and two young children waking up at night; he went to work tired each morning. Eventually, we agreed to put the two boys into one bedroom and he moved into the third bedroom. I understood the need for us to sleep separately and there did not seem to be any alternative, but I did feel a sense of rejection, and that inevitably created a fault line in our marriage.

Despite sleeping apart, we had a fairly normal family life, with two intelligent and good-natured boys who were our pride and joy. We loved the two boys dearly and, whilst there were no big Christmas presents or foreign holidays, we had great fun during their early years, spending weekends and summer holidays in a farm in the Mournes that Trudy rented from the Keown family. It was an ancient two-bedroom cottage with no hot water or heating, but the massive fireplace kept us toasty most of the time. The boys loved roaming in Tollymore Forest Park in their brightly coloured Wellington boots, making sandcastles on Cranfield beach or having picnics up in the hills. One very hot day, while the boys were playing with other children in the shallow water at the edge of the lake in Tollymore, Owen, aged only about two or three, fell and got soaked to the skin. Conall, ever the loving and caring elder brother, took off his t-shirt for Owen to wear, but it went down to almost his knees and a few people mistook him for a little girl in a dress. Owen was not amused.

The boys also enjoyed helping on the farm with the two Keown children, Thomas and Jennifer, particularly at lambing season, when they could feed the lambs who had been abandoned by the ewes. Thomas, being the oldest, was like a pack leader and my boys looked up to him. Many years later I met Thomas in the Irish Association in Boston, USA, while I spent a week in Boston College during my master's-degree course. The Irish Association was the mirror image of the CWA in Belfast, helping new immigrants in their host country. I was the CWA's director then.

In July 1987 my brother Henry and I took the boys to Hong Kong to visit the Lo family. Henry had become a senior engineer with Marconi and kindly paid the fare for one of the boys; I saved enough money from interpreting for the other two fares. Conall, at five, and Owen, at two, had never been on a plane before. Conall asked the pilots to autograph his diary for the trip and they put in it a flight map with their best wishes and signatures, which delighted Conall and helped break the tedium of the long flight. Much as I like going to Hong Kong, the long journey is always exhausting. I was proud of the two of them, behaving impeccably while enjoying the excitement of their first experience of flying. It was wonderful for Mother to meet her two bright and handsome grandsons for the first time, but I could see that she had lost a lot of weight and looked tired. For some months she had been seeing a doctor, who had diagnosed indigestion. This was proven some years later to be a misdiagnosis.

We stayed in the flat with Mother for three weeks, with visits to see my siblings – who, by then, all had their own homes. My oldest brother, David, and his family had moved into Taikoo Shing, a large-scale middle-class private residential development built on a vacant dockland in Quarry Bay, with apartments, landscaped gardens, sports facilities and restaurants. I was glad it was so convenient for Mother – it was just the next district to North Point.

Eddie, Lisa and their lovely eight-year-old daughter, Edith, had moved to the Mid-Levels on the south side of Hong Kong Island, to a place with a commanding view of the sea. It was a bit far from North Point but Eddie had a car and would collect Mother often for dinner in their apartment. Mary and her partner had just set up their own business and lived with his parents in a spacious apartment in Kowloon. The boys loved visiting Auntie Mary in her luxurious home, with little Owen jumping on the massive leather sofa.

Despite the stifling midsummer tropical heat, the boys had a wonderful time being taken out to places of interest and were fascinated by the Ocean Park, the Peak Tram, the Space Museum, the Buddhist temples, the vast shopping malls and the state-of-the-art restaurants, including a new revolving eatery in a skyscraper, where they took an outside lift almost up into the clouds.

This was the third time I had visited Hong Kong since I left in 1974 and each time I was amazed by the dramatic changes in the place. It had become a modern, cosmopolitan, vibrant and prosperous city, offering many exciting opportunities. I was glad to see all my siblings doing well. My mother, although looking thin, was well cared for by the family close by. Before we left we had a family photograph taken in a studio, the last and the only one with all of us present except David – three generations of the Lo family.

8

Returning to Part-time Work and Studies

When Owen started playgroup in 1987, I began working part-time in the CWA, which had been set up by the Chinese Chamber of Commerce a year earlier under a government scheme to tackle long-term unemployment. Based in premises owned by the Chamber of Commerce in Eblana Street in south Belfast, the CWA aimed to provide advice and assistance to Chinese people and to help them access public services. The scheme had a coordinator, Eleanor McKnight, and some ten staff, whose posts were only funded for a year. I joined initially as an English-language tutor but became a community interpreter when some separate funding became available.

Those four years spent helping Chinese people to see GPs, hospital doctors, social workers and other professionals deepened my understanding of how the language barrier affected their lives. Most of them were Hakka Chinese, the indigenous people of Hong Kong, who had traditionally made their living from small farms in rural areas. However, as refugees began to arrive in Hong Kong from communist China from 1949 onwards, bringing with them immense wealth and skills, the city began to prosper and demand for imported food soared. The local small farms were unable to compete with bulk buying from the USA or Australia and went into decline. With limited education and qualifications, these farmers stood little chance of securing jobs in the city either and, when the British government opened its doors during the postwar economic boom, many left the villages to seek a better life in the UK.

Unlike the UK, Hong Kong had very limited free public services at the time and virtually no social-benefit system. The new immigrants coming to Northern Ireland in the sixties and seventies had no idea about what public services were available to them and there were no translated leaflets. This was in contrast with bigger cities such as London or Birmingham, which were fast becoming cosmopolitan places and provided plenty of help and advice for new immigrants. For those with little command of English, particularly women, getting to see a doctor often depended on persuading someone else – one of their children or a friend – to go with them to interpret. I heard of a child aged four who helped his mum to speak to her GP. The first one in the family to learn English, the child had picked the language up at nursery school. This situation not only diminished the right of the women involved to confidentiality about their health issues but also placed an enormous burden of responsibility on the children. With their lack of language skills and qualifications, nearly all of Northern Ireland's Chinese immigrants were confined to working in the Chinese-catering trade, which did not help them to improve their English or integrate into the wider society.

The absence of family support and unsocial working hours in

My parents' wedding in 1938.

My father, Lo Ping-Fai.

My mother, Wai Kam-Ping.

The North Point Estate in Hong Kong where I grew up.

With my younger sister, Mary, in the North Point Estate.

With Mary in 1956.

Me, second from left, with primary school friends, sitting on a small cannon in the local park.

The prefects with our teacher Miss Cheung, taken in 1967. I'm on the far left.

On a boating trip with my best friend, Bu Shiu Fun, in 1970.

On holiday in Taiwan, 1972.

With Denis at St Stephen's Beach, Hong Kong, *c.*1970.

At Kai Tak airport in January 1974 with my eldest brother David and his wife Lulu.

And with my mother and my sister Mary.

With David on our wedding day, 7 October 1974.

Our wedding party (L–R): Maureen Tattersall (David's aunt), Gerry Hegan (David's aunt), Trudy (David's mother), David, me, my brother Eddie, our best man Craig and David's brother Nicholas.

takeaways caused not only childcare problems but also isolation – again, particularly for women – and family disharmony. Soon after taking on the part-time interpreter's position, I set up a weekly mother-and-toddler group in the CWA to enable young and lonely mothers to get together. I knew how the mother-and-toddler group I used to attend had helped me to feel less isolated. I had some toys belonging to my own two boys but I asked friends and neighbours for their old toys too. Within a fortnight, my front room was filled with dolls, toy prams, toy cars, jigsaw puzzles, books and so on. The BBC's Save the Children Fund also gave us a grant so that we could buy bigger items such as an indoor slide, a table and some chairs. One evening, though, the premises were broken into and the heartless burglars took away most of our toys and equipment. We had to start gathering stuff all over again.

A recent film, *The Lady in the Van*, reminded me of a case I worked on in conjunction with social services. We were to section a mentally ill Chinese man who had lived alone in a derelict house with no electricity and heating in Newry for ten years, scavenging food from discarded produce in rubbish bins at the local market. He had been a designer and printer in Hong Kong and had moulded and painted a beautiful mural inside his house, depicting an ancient landscape. He put up no resistance when the social worker, a GP, the police and I, as their interpreter, arrived in darkness in his house to take him away under the Mental Health Act. We need not have worried about having to drag him out, kicking and screaming. In fact, he was very grateful to be taken away and cared for by the health and social services – a happy ending.

My low-paid part-time hours in CWA were woefully inadequate for a job that involved covering interpreting sessions all over Northern Ireland, and at times I was running up over a hundred hours of unpaid overtime, but the health trusts refused to extend my paid hours. Under the shadow of the overwhelming sectarian conflict that consumed the attention of both the government and the media, the needs of minority-ethnic residents were falling under the radar of public consciousness.

Before joining the CWA, when I had been at home full time with the kids, I had gone back to studying at evening classes again and had obtained more O-level and A-level qualifications. I was particularly proud that I had got A grades for English language and literature. It was a natural progression, then, to take on a six-year part-time degree in general studies at Queen's University, Belfast, while I worked in the CWA. After my first year, I was offered a place to study full time for a degree in anthropology, a subject I found really interesting (and apparently I had come top in the examination in that module), but I turned it down. The children were still very young and I needed the wages from the CWA.

However, in 1991, at the end of my second year at Queen's, Belfast's social-work training body persuaded me to embark on a two-year social-work course at the University of Ulster. Having worked as the CWA's part-time community interpreter for four years, I had been assisting a number of Chinese families and individuals who were involved with social services and I realised that there was a great need for a dedicated Chinese social worker who understood the culture and spoke the language.

Despite the fact that the Department of Health and Social Services (DHSS) had agreed not only to pay for the tuition fees but also to give me a cost-of-living grant equivalent to my CWA wages, David was not keen on the idea. He argued that none of the wives of his colleagues and friends was in full-time education. His prevarication did surprise and annoy me, particularly since he knew I had left school against my will and had always longed for more education and a professional qualification that could lead to a good career. Fortunately, a colleague of his informed him how much a qualified social worker earned, which eventually persuaded him to cooperate in completing the necessary grant form verifying his income for me to proceed. I gave up the general-studies course at Queen's and, in September 1991, started my diploma in social work at the Jordanstown campus of the University of Ulster.

Conall, by then aged nine, and Owen, aged six, were well established in school. David and I finished work and lectures fairly early in the afternoon, so the boys were not with the childminder for long each day. David helped the boys with their homework and got dinner ready on weekdays.

At the beginning of October, just a week or two after I had begun the course, Eddie called me from Hong Kong, breaking the news that Mother had been diagnosed with pancreatic cancer, which her doctor had for several years mistaken for indigestion. Mother had often complained about her stomach to me in her letters and when we visited her in Hong Kong, but I had not expected this. Mother and I used to write regularly, at least once a fortnight, and on occasions such as Chinese New Year I would telephone her, but international calls were expensive and, with the time difference (Hong Kong is seven or eight hours ahead of the UK), trying to arrange a mutually convenient time added another layer of restriction. Gradually, with my own family and my studies, even the correspondence became less frequent, although I always sent her photographs of her two grandsons to keep her abreast of their development.

Eddie said that she was going to have surgery to help relieve the pressure on her stomach, but that it would not remove the growth.

'It is terminal,' he said, 'but doctors don't know, at this stage, how long she has left.'

I talked to my tutor. Although he sympathised, he said they could only give me two weeks' leave to visit my mother. Any longer than that and I might be asked to repeat my first year, which could jeopardise my funding. I was terrified of losing my place, having gone through a stiff entrance competition and all that hassle from David.

I thought about it, wanting to go to see her but unsure whether, if I got there and saw her condition getting worse, I could bear to leave at the end of my two-week stay. David left the decision entirely to me. I consulted with my brother Henry in Coventry and we both decided to wait until after the operation.

The operation went well and made her more comfortable. My sister, Mary, kept us updated about her progress over the phone, with Henry and I both preparing to fly over soon. She was discharged to Eddie's home but, within days, deteriorated rapidly and was readmitted to hospital. She died very soon afterwards, on 29 October – suddenly but, thankfully, without pain.

Devastated, I kicked myself for being so indecisive in those few weeks. I should have dropped everything and gone to see her immediately after I had heard from Eddie; I should have followed my heart rather than my head. It remains one of the biggest regrets in my life. Henry had been just about to book a flight home and was inconsolable, too, on hearing the news. He and I did not go back for the funeral. There was no point; it was too late. I excused myself from lectures on the day of my mother's funeral and lit some incense sticks to feel part of the ritual back home. Linda, our wonderful childminder and neighbour, came with a large bouquet of roses and I sobbed on her shoulder in uncontrollable grief.

With a heavy heart, I threw myself into the university-based course, which was intensive. There were three work placements packed into the two years, with one placement during the summer months. My three placements were quite varied, giving me a taste of working in different settings. The first, to ease me in, was in a school; for the second I went to a probation hostel in south Belfast from July to September; and the final placement was with Shankill Social Services.

The hostel placement was tough. The majority of the clients had been referred there as a bail condition while they awaited trial, or had just been released from imprisonment for sexual crimes. Like other staff, I had to cover shifts supervising the residents twenty-four hours a day. One morning, when I reported for duty, I was told to take a woman to another hostel across the city. She had been violent to another resident the night before and was being expelled. She slumped beside me in the passenger seat of my car, looking rather sleepy.

'Poor you,' I said. 'You must not have had much sleep last night.'

She mumbled something incoherent in response. Then I realised that she was actually drifting in and out of consciousness. She confessed that she had taken an overdose of drugs before leaving the hostel. There was no time to lose. I turned the car round and, not caring about speed, headed straight to the Royal Victoria Hospital and shouted for help at the door. The woman had her stomach pumped and, thankfully, recovered.

I graduated in June 1993 as the first ever trained social worker from an ethnic-minority background in Northern Ireland. The plan was to convince social services to create a dedicated post in which I could work with families from the Chinese community. But this proved to be too complex. It was disappointing – we knew there was need for a post like that, given the number of cases on the books of social services. Instead, I got a job immediately after graduation in the family and childcare section of Newtownards Social Services on a temporary contract, but I hoped it would become permanent. During my first week, a senior social worker called me into her office. She asked me gingerly, 'Anna, I have to be careful how to put this across to you. I was thinking … would you agree to us seeking consent from clients before we assign you as their social worker?' She added for emphasis, 'After all, the trust promotes client choice.'

Taken totally aback, I told her that, if she did that, clients would expect problems when there were none. It was hard to comprehend that a senior colleague viewed me as different from my white peers and had doubts as to whether I would be acceptable to local clients. It was blatant racism, particularly incompatible with the much-emphasised social-work values of embracing diversity and anti-discriminatory practice. I could have complained to the authorities but did not wish to rock the boat as a new social worker. I left as soon as I could and went to work for Bangor Social Services.

With me back in full-time work and earning a decent wage, we went to the Canary Islands that summer for our first family holiday abroad. The four of us enjoyed two weeks' blazing sunshine and the Spanish cuisine. With some persistence, I also managed to persuade David to move house. We got a much bigger and nicely renovated house in Cyprus Park, a quiet leafy street in east Belfast, not far from our flat in Cyprus Avenue. It was just in time to have a party for our twentieth wedding anniversary in October 1994.

The boys were delighted to have their own bedrooms instead of sharing one and Owen was able to walk to Strandtown Primary School, just around the corner. Working in Bangor was handy, too, as Conall had just started in Sullivan Upper School in Holywood. In the morning I dropped him off on the way to my office and he went home on the school bus. Both boys loved school; they were academically able but also enjoyed sports and extra-curricular activities. Conall was crowned the school chess champion in primary six, overtaking all the older boys and girls in the chess club. We were pleased, too, that they were well-behaved pupils and popular among teachers and classmates. Conall was excellent at all science subjects but particularly brilliant at mathematics, winning UK-wide recognition, while Owen was creative and artistic, perhaps taking that from me. I was very proud that his sketch of a house plant became the back cover of the school magazine when he was in primary six. He was very active in the Cubs and later the Scouts, earning dozens and dozens of badges over the years (all diligently sewn onto his shirt and campfire blanket by his obliging mother). Conall became a mountain-bike enthusiast from the time he was about twelve years of age until he left home to attend the University of Nottingham in England.

Meanwhile, it was a tough job working in family and childcare. I had a heavy workload and lots of responsibilities. Indeed, it would have been a very steep learning curve for any newly qualified social worker. Thankfully, my superiors in Bangor – particularly the team leader, Jenny McLaughlin – were wise and supportive. I had a colleague whom I found dismissive of me and, when she made racist remarks towards some clients, a Chinese family, I complained to Jenny, who dealt with the problem firmly and fairly. Of course, I made mistakes too. It was all part of learning and gaining experience.

There were a few hair-raising moments. One day I walked into a home to find a female client being held hostage by her ex-partner, who had just been released from prison and had tracked her down to her new home in a social-housing estate in Holywood. We escaped, as he was hiding upstairs, and got into my car, which was parked across the road. On realising the woman had left the house, the ex-partner dashed out and ran towards us. I shouted to my client to lock her door. He tried to yank it open while I started the engine. Then he moved to stand in front of my car, pushing against the bonnet while I began to move; I continued to drive forward, daring him to back off. He then jumped onto the bonnet, holding on to my windscreen wipers. I kept driving and, finally, he jumped off.

I took her to the police station in the High Street to report the incident but, just as we were about to leave, this rascal of a man arrived on foot, to our horror. He was planning to report the incident to the police before we did. Later I realised that, while my client had locked her door, I had not locked mine – there was no central locking in my 1990s Peugeot. Had the man come to my side of the door, he could have opened it and dragged me out. My sons loved this story – it sounded like something from a James Bond movie to them – but my supervisors were alarmed to hear that I had been trying to run over a civilian in the middle of a housing estate.

There were many sad stories, too. I took one two-and-a-half-year-old boy into care one morning after a whole week spent attempting to gain access to check on him. On the one hand we were trying to help his mother to stay off drink and care for him properly so as to be able to keep him, and on the other hand we were carrying out our statutory duty to ensure the wellbeing of the child. At the end of that week, I called very early in the morning, just before 8 a.m. The mother opened the door in a drunken state, admitting to not having answered the door for five days because she had been drinking. I found the toddler in his cot, soaked in filth. I took him downstairs, suspecting he was hungry, got him a bowl of cereal and watched him eat like a starved animal. We placed him in foster care. He was diagnosed with depression at the tender age of three – probably caused by the severe neglect of his mother, who clearly loved him but was sadly under the control of alcohol.

In 1995, Barnardo's Tuar Ceatha Services set up the Chinese Health Project in partnership with my previous employer, the CWA, and I left Bangor Social Services after working there for two years to become its project worker. Together with two lay health workers, we were given the core aim of identifying the health needs of the Chinese and Vietnamese-Chinese communities and providing culturally specific health initiatives. We managed casework, helping families to see health professionals, learn parenting skills, draw up household budgets, attend parent–teacher meetings and access welfare benefits. We also facilitated the two women's groups, Oi Kwan (meaning 'gregarious') in Belfast and Oi Wah (meaning 'love of all things Chinese') in Craigavon, which had been set up with the project's help. We brought together very isolated women and helped them provide support for each other and develop self-confidence. The Oi Kwan Women's Group has thrived beyond expectation. It is now a well-established group with expertise in Chinese and modern dancing, fundraising for charities and running social events. The chair, Selina Lee, received a well-deserved MBE for her services to the Chinese community.

Just before I joined, the lay health workers conducted surveys of fifty Chinese families in each of the two areas, identifying their health needs. My first piece of work was to write up a report based on this survey. It was one of the first published reports on the Chinese community and received some publicity. My previous colleague, Seamus McKee, conducted a sympathetic interview with me on the Radio Ulster morning news programme. I was critical of the health authorities' neglect of this section of their community, not providing them with proper information or assistance in accessing NHS services. Many of them had never been to a dentist and were totally unaware of other health provisions such as physiotherapy. With no prior knowledge of the UK social-benefit system, some of them had never applied for child benefit or other welfare entitlements and had lost out on thousands of pounds over the years.

Apart from the health project, I also supervised a community-development project in north Belfast, working with a women's group to help them gain training and employment with the support of a Barnardo's crèche.

The Tuar Ceatha Services, headed by a project leader, Pauline Leeson, had been working closely with travellers' projects, the CWA and the Indian community in the long campaign for the introduction of a racial anti-discrimination law in Northern Ireland. During my two years in Barnardo's I became more and more involved in lobbying for racial-equality legislation for ethnic minorities.

9

The Campaign for Race-relations Legislation, 1990–7

When I first mentioned to Chinese people I knew that I had found local people generally very friendly – in spite of one unpleasant incident of a minor assault by a punk in a Belfast street – I realised their experiences were very different to mine. The difference, they suggested, was due to the 'polite, middle-class circles' I moved in.

By the 1980s, the Chinese community had become the largest ethnic minority in Northern Ireland, with an estimated population of nearly eight thousand and several hundred catering outlets throughout the region. However, the language barrier had rendered them 'deaf and dumb', as some had said, with many having difficulty getting information and availing of health, housing and other public services. The lack of integration had also resulted in a sense of alienation and isolation. Racist harassment was a fact of life for many of them, interacting with local people on a daily basis in their catering businesses, with frequent and persistent occurrences ranging from verbal abuse to minor or serious vandalism. Some related to me incidents of their shops being pelted with eggs, tomatoes and even stones; of broken windows; of cars being damaged or burnt out. I was shocked to hear that some Chinese women thought that being spat at by young children was a western custom.

Moreover, many were reluctant to report incidents to the police for fear of drawing attention and attracting further harassment. It saddened me to feel their sense of helplessness. They accepted it as inevitable that they would face discrimination and endure second-class-citizen status in the UK, as this was not their home country. I remember when I first spoke of racism in the media, some Chinese elders chided me: 'Anna, don't talk about racism here. Don't sound so angry. You only annoy the locals, saying that they hassle us. This is not our homeland – of course we will be bullied.'

My reply to them was, 'There are plenty of good people here who will be on our side and support us. But if we don't tell them, they won't know and we will be letting the bullies get away with it!'

There were also local people who criticised me for speaking out about racism, fearing that any publicity in this regard would further damage Northern Ireland's image, which was already in tatters following years of violence. One friend said, 'For goodness sake, Anna, we are bad enough with our reputation for sectarianism without you banging on about racism as well!'

With our own two sons, Conall and Owen, we witnessed racial bullying in schools and summer schemes, as well as unprovoked racist abuse in public places from youngsters not much older than them. Conall encountered racist bullying in the first days of primary school – a quiet little feeder school in leafy, suburban east Belfast. He was harassed in the playground by a primary-two boy and did not understand why he was being targeted. Initially, we were reluctant to approach the school. We did not want to seem like over-anxious, complaining parents and we thought it might settle down with time. However, it went on and on. After some weeks, we wrote a letter for Conall to take into school and give to the teacher, requesting a meeting to discuss a problem he was experiencing. Later that day, as usual, I waited for Conall after school with the other parents. The teacher came out into the playground, with all the primary-one pupils running down the steps to meet their waiting mums and dads. Standing at the top of the steps, in front of all the pupils and parents, the teacher asked me what it was that I wished to talk to her about. She did not invite me to go inside for a private conversation. I stuttered out an explanation of the situation and she said that she had actually noticed it. She thought it was all right – your son 'gives as good as he gets' she told me (I interpreted this as meaning that he hit back). I felt that my concerns had been totally dismissed and walked away feeling two inches tall.

Two days later, this same boy tripped Conall up on purpose in the playground, resulting in a bloody nose that dripped for twenty-four hours, and a black eye. To try to lighten the seriousness of the assault, we affectionately called it his 'panda eye', like his adored soft toy from his Hong Kong granny. It was only then that the school took action. They cordoned off a corner of the playground for the primary-one pupils and had a member of staff supervise them.

Three years later, Owen went to the same school and was picked on as well. This time we knew to alert the school principal at once. Thankfully, they reacted immediately against the offending boy, although in a way that we thought was somewhat over the top. There was no policy on racist bullying from the Department of Education at the time and the headteachers seemed to make up their own procedures as they went along.

On one occasion I took Owen, aged four and a half, for a summer outing to Crawfordsburn beach with the young Chinese children and their mums from the CWA mother-and-toddler group. While they were playing at the edge of the water, some local boys pelted them with pebbles, cutting the ear of a little Chinese girl and frightening the others. Owen said to us that evening, 'I don't want to be a Chinese boy any more. People call you names and throw stones at you if you are Chinese.' It nearly broke my heart.

It is sad to reflect that during Conall and Owen's early childhood, although they were accepted by most of their peers, incidents of racist behaviour almost invariably happened to them whenever they joined a new school or activity scheme. After Conall was attacked by three boys from another school in the street one afternoon on his way home, we sent our two young sons, then aged about eight and five, to self-defence classes to help them feel empowered and reassured that, if they should ever find themselves in a difficult situation like that again, at least they could get away.

In those days, people in Northern Ireland generally denied the existence of racism. The situation was summed up by a 1995 BBC2 documentary, entitled *The Hidden Troubles*. It was often said that there was no problem with racism here as we had so few black people. People spoke about ethnic minorities as if they brought racism with them when they arrived. Racism in Northern Ireland is a problem originating with a small proportion of the white indigenous people – it is their negative attitude towards people of colour, whether or not there are any around.

Unlike in the rest of the UK, the Northern Ireland census did not record ethnicity until 2001. Therefore, there were no statistics about the number of black and minority-ethnic people living in the region, although estimates from representative organisations indicated that there were around 20,000 in 1997. Without a headcount, it was easy for the Northern Ireland Office to play the numbers card and argue against the need for race-equality legislation.

Unlike the rest of the UK, where race-relations legislation had been in place since the 1960s, culminating in the 1976 Race Relations Act, Northern Ireland had no race-discrimination law until 1997. We were twenty-one years behind England, Wales and Scotland. Again, it was the myth that there were very few black people in Northern Ireland, and thus very little racism, that had allowed Westminster to justify not extending the act to Northern Ireland in the 1970s. In fact, this argument is nonsense. The smaller the ethnic-minority population, the less likely they are to have formal or informal networks to turn to for support when they encounter problems – and the more they need statutory protection.

It took a seven-year campaign to successfully lobby for the Race Relations Act to be extended to Northern Ireland. It was widely accepted that the advent of race legislation to Northern Ireland was mostly the result of effective lobbying and the mobilisation of ethnic-minority groups, civil-liberties bodies and voluntary organisations, rather than of leadership from Westminster or any political motivation on the part of the local unionist and nationalist parties.

The drive for change began with the travellers' support movement in the late 1980s, highlighting racism against travellers. This struck a chord with other minority-ethnic groups, even though they were mostly in the embryonic stage of their own development then. The Committee for the Administration of Justice (CAJ), a civil-liberties group, took the lead in partnership with the travellers' projects, the CWA, the Indian Community Centre and other minority-ethnic groups in campaigning for anti-racist legislation in Northern Ireland.

In 1991 a landmark conference, Racism in Northern Ireland, was held in Belfast. There was a great turnout of attendees from ethnic-minority communities, government departments and voluntary organisations. I spoke on the experiences of Chinese people and my speech was well received. A woman came up to me afterwards to tell me that I made her cry when I had related the racist episodes against my own children. A conference report was produced, with three key demands: the establishment of a commission for racial equality, the passing of anti-racist legislation and the inclusion of travellers as an ethnic-minority group in any such legislation.

With expert input from CAJ, the campaign was extended to try to bring international pressure to bear on the British government. In 1993 I went with Martin O'Brien from CAJ and Paul Noonan from the Belfast Travellers' Education and Development Group to Geneva, the UN's European headquarters, to lobby politicians from member states during one of their three-yearly meetings on racial equality, naming and shaming the British government for their inaction in Northern Ireland. Martin, intelligent and articulate, was no stranger to Geneva and we arrived the weekend ahead of the scheduled meeting to do some sightseeing. We strolled along the beautiful Lake Geneva with its dramatic water jet and visited some of the historic buildings and monuments in this hub of commerce and finance, including the Reformation Wall. Attending the UN with veterans in campaigning was very useful for me – I learned how to approach politicians to make our case and try to win their hearts and minds.

In 1994, we saw the birth of the Northern Ireland Council for Ethnic Minorities (NICEM), set up to represent various migrant communities and focus on the fight for legislation. Suneil Sharma from the Indian community and I were elected its chair and vice-chair respectively. Patrick Yu was later appointed director. Being quite unfamiliar with the workings of committees, I was able to learn from people who had been working in the voluntary sector for some time. Eventually, in July 1996, draft race legislation was introduced and Westminster enacted the Race Relations (Northern Ireland) Order in August 1997. The Commission for Racial Equality for Northern Ireland was created shortly afterwards. Grass-roots coalition lobbying had brought some significant results.

There was jubilation in minority-ethnic communities that they would now be protected by law from discrimination in employment, the provision of services and the provision of facilities. No one could now turn anyone down for a job on grounds of race; no one could turn anyone away from renting a home or business premises on grounds of race. More importantly, all statutory services would now be made accessible to ethnic-minority residents. There was a satisfying sense of achievement and pride among us. It was a triumph that had arisen from a community movement.

Despite the fact that they had not fought for it, many of the political parties welcomed the new legislation. The Alliance Party and the SDLP thought that the order did not go far enough, in fact, although the DUP and the Ulster Unionist Party (UUP) were unhappy that the legislation went so far as to have included travellers. It seemed typical to us that our political parties were unable to agree on anything.

10

Developing the CWA, 1997–2007

The extension of race-relations law to Northern Ireland brought about a sea-change in statutory attitudes and policies towards ethnic-minority people in the region, placing a duty on the government and local authorities to make all public information and services accessible to ethnic minorities. The cross-departmental Racial Equality Strategy and the Racial Equality Commission materialised within a year or so afterwards.

In the last two years of the campaign, I was working in Barnardo's, supervising two projects. As a UK-wide and longstanding charity, Barnardo's in Belfast was well structured, with a loyal and professional staff. I learned a great deal from the organisation as a whole, but most of all from the Tuar Ceatha Services leader, Pauline Leeson, who not only was instrumental in the race-legislation campaign but also spearheaded a number of projects for ethnic minorities, including the Chinese Health Project I was involved in and a significant piece of research entitled *Out of the Shadows*, which appeared in 1995. I could not have asked for a better mentor from whom to learn about rights and evidence-based approaches to racial equality, as well as the workings of statutory and voluntary organisations.

In Barnardo's I worked closely with the CWA on the Chinese Health Project. Having worked in the CWA previously as its community interpreter, I knew the organisation well – both its strengths and weaknesses. It had been established in 1986 under the government's Action for Community Employment (ACE) Scheme to provide short-term training and employment opportunities in community settings for the long-term unemployed. The ACE structure was utterly inappropriate for the CWA, which struggled to find enough unemployed Chinese people to fill the nine low-paid posts year on year. Although the coordinator of the project was always a permanent position in order to maintain stability, the constant changes in the other staff led to a lack of continuity in CWA services and facilities and, crucially, hampered the organisation's own development. Despite its precarious funding position, the CWA was very fortunate in having two very able coordinators in its first ten years.

The first coordinator, Eleanor McKnight, who hailed from Omagh and had taught English overseas, was pivotal in involving the CWA in the race-legislation campaign. When the Northern Ireland Office provided funding for Eleanor to become a race-relations officer in the CWA in 1992, Deborah Gadd, who had been a part-time English tutor there, took over as its new coordinator.

The ineffectual ACE programme soon started to be phased out and, by 1996, the CWA had to look elsewhere for enough funding to stay afloat. Deborah, from Bangor, a language graduate of Trinity College, Dublin, was most effective in sourcing alternative funding for a number of community-development posts in 1996. She then moved to head up the CWA's new community-development team of three.

In 1996, the CWA published a four-year development plan, setting out its vision. This included the need for a Chinese sheltered-housing scheme and a dedicated community centre. Another of the recommendations was the appointment of a director, who should be a member of the Chinese community. The DHSS agreed to fund the position for three years.

It was not an easy decision for me to apply for the position of director when it was advertised. There were obvious risks in moving from a permanent position in Barnardo's to a not-much-known community organisation for a time-limited post. David, naturally, had reservations about it, but understood my ambition for the organisation. By this time our sons were aged fifteen and twelve and well settled in Sullivan Upper School.

I got the job and started in June 1997, with the Race Relations Order about to be enacted in Westminster and Tony Blair having just won a landslide victory for the Labour Party after seventeen years of Conservative rule. The future looked bright.

I spent ten satisfying years working with the able and committed staff team in developing the CWA and working with the Chinese community. Strange as it may sound, I probably achieved many more tangible outcomes in the CWA than in my nine years as an elected representative in the Northern Ireland Assembly. I also fulfilled my yearning for education, obtaining a diploma in management and a master's degree in organisational leadership by studying part time in the University of Ulster, which I hope I put to good use.

It must be said, though, that I came back to the CWA as its director at an optimal time, with an unprecedented, glowing scenario of exciting new opportunities and resources. Deservedly, minority-ethnic communities were reaping the fruits of the long-fought campaign for the introduction of the Race Relations Order. And soon there was another tool at their disposal. The Good Friday Agreement and the subsequent Northern Ireland Act 1998 also placed a statutory duty on all government departments, agencies and councils to promote equality of opportunity and good community relations among all groupings in the province. The Assembly returned in 1998 made commitments to various policies to tackle racial inequality and targeted support towards ethnic-minority groups. With the Chinese community the largest minority-ethnic group in Northern Ireland, the CWA found itself not only pushing at open doors but actually inundated by collaboration requests from public bodies.

With the ceasefires, Northern Ireland had finally come out of the Troubles. People were greatly optimistic that we were returning to normality, without the orange-and-green sectarian conflict plaguing society and dominating political and media foci. Ethnic-minority issues finally began to register in politicians' minds and journalists were eager to find new angles and emerging social topics from a region rising out of years of darkness into a new light. In 1998 and 1999 the media included the Chinese community and the CWA in a range of coverage. Even newspapers in the Republic of Ireland and Hong Kong wrote about us. I negotiated with my previous employer, the BBC, to have a programme in Cantonese piloted in 1998 – which, although somewhat tokenistic at only five minutes a week, was a gesture of goodwill.

The EU began to inject billions of euros into Northern Ireland in the mid-1990s to consolidate the peace process under its Programme for Peace and Reconciliation. The CWA was quick to act and benefited from the various strands and phases of the PEACE money. However, longer-lasting security came from setting up projects in interpreting, advocacy and support for the elderly in the CWA, with permanent funding from health and social-care trusts in Belfast and Derry-Londonderry that has continued until today. I am proud to say that the annual income of the CWA increased almost fourfold between 1997 and its peak in 2006, a year before I left the organisation.

With proper resourcing in place, I set about making the organisation more professional – improving internal policies and structures, revising employment terms and introducing systems for staff development. As a result, we got a well-qualified and dedicated team with a recognised pay scale and pension scheme, supported by staff supervision and training. All of this led to our being awarded Investors in People recognition. It was often a multicultural mix of staff – Chinese people from mainland China, Hong Kong and Malaysia, Canadians, Polish people and Northern Irish men and women from both sides of the political divide. There was a friendly atmosphere in the office and great camaraderie between staff, some of whom have now moved on to positions in statutory agencies or qualified in social work. One of our wonderful staff, Leish Dolan, helped a particular Chinese woman, Stella Tsang, who had limited English, to become a most valuable CWA volunteer by pairing up with her for cultural-awareness training. Stella is now a freelance contributor to cultural events and Leish is a Good-Relations officer in Belfast City Council. They are both doing great work in promoting community relations.

We enabled Chinese people to establish community groups, women's groups and other interest groups all over Northern Ireland. By 2007 there were twenty-seven such groups. We set up the Wah Hep Chinese Community Association in Craigavon, which has since become independent of the CWA, and the Sai Pak Chinese Community Association in Derry-Londonderry, which the CWA still manages. These are like mini-CWAs, providing interpreting, advocacy and other services and networking with statutory agencies, councils and voluntary organisations to promote mutual understanding and integration.

Through many of these community groups we conducted needs assessments in different localities – the health and housing needs of elderly Chinese residents; the needs of Chinese young people; the mental-health needs of the Chinese community in Belfast. We also collaborated with other agencies in research initiatives regarding racism, volunteering, education, training, service provision, voting and other issues. From a total dearth of statistics about minority-ethnic people, we saw a sudden rush to identify their needs and improve inclusivity in order to fulfil new statutory obligations – all of which, of course, we welcomed.

In the CWA, we created and expanded a range of service provision for Chinese people, including interpreting, welfare rights and immigration advice, health advocacy, support for the elderly,

English-language teaching, pre-school playgroups, after-school clubs and other youth activities. Some second-generation young people who took part in our youth projects are now CWA staff or on the Management Committee. In later years we set up IT classes and, in partnership with others, training for childminders and care assistants, in order to widen employment prospects for Chinese people. My brother Henry, after being made redundant from his job as a senior computer engineer in Marconi when the company collapsed, returned to Northern Ireland and applied successfully for the position of coordinator for our new IT project. He helped to teach computer technology to hundreds of Chinese people, young and old. Some learned to use the internet and email in their eighties.

Perhaps the widest impact the CWA had in those years was in raising awareness about the needs of the minority-ethnic population, particularly the Chinese community, thereby influencing public- and social-policy development to be more inclusive. Our race-relations officers also conducted anti-racism training for the public, private and voluntary sectors, as well as in schools, colleges, universities and youth projects.

We lobbied government ministers, MLAs and councillors. Various secretaries of state – Peter Mandelson, Mo Mowlam, John Reid – graced the CWA with their attendance for our Chinese-new-year celebrations and other events. Another secretary of state, Peter Hain, wrote the foreword for the CWA's twentieth-anniversary publication in 2006, paying tribute to our work in 'fostering the integration of Chinese people into wider civic society and indeed in helping form that civic society, by acting as the "voice of the Chinese community'". In 2001, more than thirty MLAs, including four government ministers, attended our colourful Chinese-New-Year reception in the Long Gallery at Stormont, certainly a rare occasion. Junior ministers from the Office of the First Minister and Deputy First Minister (OFMDFM) launched our strategic plans in 2000 and in 2005, publicly endorsing the actions we planned. All such public acknowledgement helped to raise the CWA's profile and the status of the Chinese community in Northern Ireland.

We also forged alliances and partnerships with statutory bodies and voluntary organisations, playing a key role in many ethnic-minority liaison groups and committees – including those of the police, health authorities and government departments – to promote understanding of the barriers to accessing public services and to ensure that issues of equality were brought into policy development. It was gratifying that we had a positive influence on OFMDFM and on Belfast City Council in setting up grants for ethnic-minority organisations and projects, which have not only lasted but increased in value over the years. The Assembly's Minority Ethnic Development Fund now provides over £1 million a year to support organisations working with ethnic-minority communities.

Another tangible outcome was the establishment in 2004 of the Belfast Trust's Regional Interpreting Service, which largely used the CWA's Chinese interpreting service as its foundation and model. The Northern Ireland Health and Social Care Interpreting Service now provides thousands of interpreting sessions a year, covering a comprehensive range of languages for non-English-speaking residents using NHS services in hospitals, health centres, nursing homes and other settings throughout Northern Ireland. Others, such as the Police Service of Northern Ireland (PSNI), also appointed ethnic-minority liaison officers and produced translated leaflets in various languages. We even got some local libraries to stock Chinese books and magazines, to the great delight of those who could not read English.

When the Equality Commission for Northern Ireland was created in 1999, I was appointed a founding commissioner for a term of three years. I was also elected by community representatives as the first chair of the South Belfast Partnership Board under the Department of Social Development's Neighbourhood Renewal Strategy. All these positions helped the CWA to network with others and to be at the leading edge of the racial-equality agenda in Northern Ireland.

In terms of promoting cultural diversity in society, we had great fun each year staging public Chinese-New-Year celebrations in Belfast in Saint George's Market, bringing professional groups from the UK and China to perform traditional dances, acrobatics and magic shows to entertain thousands of local people of all ages. Our staff also collaborated with various groups and local councils in other locations, such as Derry-Londonderry, Craigavon, Lisburn and Carrickfergus, to celebrate Chinese New Year. The Chinese-New-Year festival is now in the civic calendar of many cities and towns in Northern Ireland. It has been a long journey and I hope we have played a vital role in its promotion. I am very glad, too, that my sons and other second-generation Chinese young people get the opportunity to enjoy a bit of

Chinese culture and arts on these occasions.

Regrettably, Conall and Owen are not bilingual, although they know a few phrases and words, such as *dim-sum* names. They were allowed to order them themselves in restaurants if they could pronounce them. I did read them lots of children's books about Chinese legends and heroes, with great illustrations, and our home always contained lots of Chinese paintings and figurines.

During my years in the CWA they grew up into bright and sociable teenagers. Conall got hooked on mountain biking and Owen loved tagging along to events and competitions at weekends with his big brother. David, himself a keen cyclist, would turn up with his bicycle and in his cycling gear now and again, but most of the time I drove the two boys, with their bikes on the rack behind the car, all over Northern Ireland and at times to the south, to different forest parks. While the young people competed against each other, riding up and down narrow muddy paths, the parents stood around, chatting. We would bring picnics and have our lunch and breaks sitting amongst trees, bluebells and birdsong in many beautiful spots previously unknown to me. Mountain biking is a wonderful sport – truly cross community and with no social-class division.

In the summer of 1998, a year after I became the director of the CWA, I was able to take Owen to Hong Kong for a holiday and to see my relations. Conall did not want to come as his GCSE results were coming out. He did extremely well, with nine A stars and As, and went on to study A levels.

Owen and I had a great time in Hong Kong. We stayed in a lovely hotel and went out and about, sightseeing, being treated to delicious dinners in fine restaurants and receiving gifts from the uncles and aunts. I was glad for Owen to meet my siblings and his cousins, Raymond and Edith. It was a full ten years since we had last visited my homeland, when my mother was still alive. On the day of our departure, Owen did not want to leave, saying, 'Why can't we stay? Why can't we live in Hong Kong?'

When Conall was seventeen, I became his matchmaker. Heather, an old friend whom I used to see a lot when Conall was a baby, rang me one evening, asking if Conall would be willing to accompany her daughter, Fiona, to her school formal. As Conall and Fiona had not seen each other since their toddler days, I was not too sure whether he would agree. Like most boys at that age, he was also a little shy. However, I went to ask him and, without any hesitation, he said, 'Yes, great!'

So, a few weeks later, while David and I went away for a weekend in Dublin (the first time we had spent a weekend without the children), Conall invited Fiona and her friends and some of the Sullivan boys home for a party. A few couples were matched up for the girls' school formal and a romance between Conall and Fiona soon developed. Both sets of parents were delighted, although we did not know if it was to last, as they were both heading to separate universities in England soon.

We all love recognition and I was pleased when I received a MBE for services to ethnic-minority communities in 1999. The two successive chairs of the CWA Management Committee, Shek Yung Lee and Danny Wong, as well as the chairperson of the Oi Kwan Women's Group, Selina Lee, all received honours from 2001 onwards. The CWA also received an award from the

Community Foundation for Northern Ireland and Danny and I proudly accepted the trophy at a glittering gala dinner in 2005.

However, a more substantial achievement for me was the building of the Chinese sheltered-housing scheme and the Chinese Resource Centre. A large majority of elderly Chinese people in Northern Ireland, mostly those who had come to the region with their adult children, spoke little or no English. Unlike in the rural areas of Hong Kong, many Chinese couples with children had limited accommodation in Northern Ireland and had no space for their elderly parents to live with them. We helped one elderly woman to move into a sheltered-housing scheme in Belfast, but the warden was constantly on the phone to our office asking us to help with interpreting. One day, the warden sounded desperate, asking me to speak to her Chinese resident: 'Please ask her why she is crying! Is she in pain?' The truth was that, being unable to communicate, the woman felt utterly isolated and lonely. She wanted to go home to live with her married son, who did not have the space to accommodate her. We saw a number of elderly Chinese people reluctantly moving to England and Scotland to avail of Chinese sheltered housing, leaving behind their families of children and grandchildren.

As a direct response to the many elderly Chinese folk who yearned for a similar scheme in Northern Ireland, we lobbied the Housing Executive and collaborated with the BIH Housing Association to create a purpose-built arrangement for them here in Belfast. The original idea was to combine a housing scheme with a resource centre for the Chinese community on the ground floor, an example we had seen in Europe. However, when BIH had got enough funding and were ready to start building, we, disappointingly, had not raised enough for the resource centre. BIH rightly went ahead with a revised plan, building a forty-one-unit Chinese sheltered-housing scheme in McAuley Street, Belfast, with some of the features and contrasting colours – red and green – of traditional Chinese dwellings. I love the two stone lions at the porch in front of the building, which are ostensibly there to guard the residents against bad *feng shui*. I believe it is the first and only sheltered-housing scheme for elderly ethnic-minority people on the island of Ireland. The units filled up within months, as our survey had indicated. I still go to visit the elderly residents now and again and they all seem happy and content to live amongst their fellow countrymen and women, sharing the same language and culture.

Building the Chinese Resource Centre was a much more protracted and difficult process, taking some twelve years and finally reaching completion in 2008, a year after I left the CWA. It was fraught with funding and site-acquisition problems. The struggle all seemed worthwhile, though, when a £1.4 million skilfully designed modern building on a prime site beside the River Lagan in south Belfast materialised. It was like magic – a dream come true.

At the beginning of the new millennium, we started fundraising for the resource centre in earnest. There was a fundraiser in Belfast City Hall, courtesy of the council, which many businesspeople and VIPs attended, including the secretary of state, John Reid, and Lady Sylvia Hermon, MP, who had been very supportive of the CWA. In addition to the £150,000 raised by the Chinese community itself, in 2006 we started to gather funding from Stormont departments, the EU PEACE Fund and the Big Lottery Fund, as well as grants from charities and businesses. By the end £1 million had been pledged, but most of the money had to be spent by 2008. It was a race against time.

Apart from raising the necessary funds, finding a suitable site in south Belfast was a big headache. We got interested in a disused mill on Donegall Pass in south Belfast, which was available at an affordable price. It was a convenient site with easy access from other parts of Northern Ireland, given that the centre would also be the base of the CWA. With the help of a technical-aid community organisation, we applied for planning permission and drew up plans for turning the building into our resource centre, complete with offices and other facilities.

However, when we consulted the local community, we faced angry opposition from a large number of residents. Some cited concerns about increased traffic, but others were less subtle, simply declaring that they feared Donegall Pass would be turned into a Chinatown if the centre were located there. Some argued that there were already too many Chinese residents in Donegall Pass and that the arrival of more Chinese people would dilute the loyalist identity of the area.

We tried to negotiate and reason with residents through their community organisation and Mediation Northern Ireland, but without much success. We could not resolve the deadlock and tensions were riding high. In fact, copies of an outrageous circular, entitled 'The Yellow Invasion' and filled with racist slurs, were distributed all around south Belfast. It stated that the local loyalist community had successfully fought off the Catholics and were now being threatened by the Chinese, who were worse. I cannot remember all of the things they said in that publication; perhaps it is better that way.

The conflict was widely publicised by the media and, being my usual stubborn self, I was quite prepared to fight it out, knowing that I would get support from other voluntary organisations ready to stand up for us and surmising that planners would not deem the objections from local residents substantial and would very likely grant us planning permission anyway. However, the CWA Management Committee was very nervous about the ongoing dispute and favoured walking away. Then I got a discreet message from the City of Belfast School of Music on Donegall Pass that a local paramilitary organisation intended to firebomb the building once it was complete. It was a real threat, even in the relative peace of 2006. We decided to look for an alternative site.

Mercifully, Belfast City Council stepped in to offer a solution that would avoid the escalation of a situation that was already gravely embarrassing to it. A senior council official came to me one morning and unfolded a map of Belfast with red circles indicating vacant council-owned land. He said, 'The council would be willing to consider leasing any of these sites to CWA if you make a strong enough case to the councillors.' We jumped at the idea. We picked a narrow site at the junction between the Ormeau Road and the embankment beside the River Lagan, overlooking the river and Ormeau Park.

The office was buzzing with excitement and anticipation as we worked up a convincing case to present to councillors during one of their monthly full council meetings. On the evening of the presentation, whilst we were waiting nervously for our team to go into the main chamber, my mobile phone rang. It was a call from my son, Conall, who was by then a pharmacist in Saint Thomas's Hospital in London, but I knew that just then he was visiting his girlfriend, Fiona, who was doing research for her PhD thesis in Dharamshala, India. I answered the phone, fearing news of an emergency. Instead, he joyously announced their engagement. It was wonderful news. I felt it was a good omen, arriving just before I marched into the chamber to deliver my pitch for the dreamed-of site. And it was – the council had agreed to grant us the lease of the site.

Following some initial difficulties with planners, we submitted an application in March 2007 with a view to getting approval in June and starting construction in September. It was tight but, given the fact that we had to spend the money by the end of the following year, we just had to keep our fingers crossed.

11

Marriage Breakup

Whilst I was devoting much of my energy to developing the CWA and raising awareness of cultural diversity in Northern Ireland, my personal life was going downhill.

By nature, my husband, David, was a shy and quiet individual with great honesty and integrity. He is one of the most honest people I have ever known. David had an unsettled childhood, and he became very anxious when he was two years old. At that time his mother, Trudy, contracted polio and was hospitalised for a year. David, meanwhile, was put into the care of his rather stern paternal grandparents in an unfamiliar environment. Trudy recovered, fortunately, although with lifelong damage to her leg. In addition, his parents' marriage was not a happy union, involving some incidents of domestic violence, which David witnessed.

His father, John, was a bank official and the family moved around Northern Ireland as John worked in different branches. They moved back to Belfast after a spell of several years in Fivemiletown, County Tyrone, so that David could attend the Royal Belfast Academic Institution after he passed the eleven-plus (the first pupil from his rural primary school to do so).

Understandably, David found it hard to fit into the new school, being all alone with a country accent and a nervous disposition. He was picked on and the episodes of bullying made him dislike the school environment. Being a very intelligent child, he did well enough academically, but he left education after his A levels to become a journalist, a career he always wanted, given his love of reading and flair for writing. He was already successfully submitting articles to newspapers on his travels as a schoolboy and was promised a reporter's position in a provincial newspaper published by the *Belfast Telegraph* if he passed his A levels. After working there for a couple of years, he joined the *Belfast Telegraph* itself at its offices on Royal Avenue, Belfast.

In stark contrast to David's childhood, mine was calm, despite the lack of material comfort. My parents were devoted and loving to each other and to us children, even though at times I felt that my father was distant. I thrived in school and, although it didn't work out, I would have been keen to take my studies further. As a young woman in Hong Kong, I was articulate, outgoing, practical and an eternal optimist. My uncles and aunts probably saw me as rather brazen, dumping a boyfriend in a steady government job to run off to London and marry a foreigner.

Interracial marriage was not that common in Hong Kong in the 1970s and there was a perception that western men tended to have many vices, such as drinking and infidelity. My parents were not able to come to our wedding, but my mother wrote soon afterwards that her home would always have an open door for me if the marriage should not work out. This was really rather liberal of my mother, as divorce in those days was taboo in Chinese society. But she loved me so much that she would rather I break the norm and return home 'in disgrace' than suffer alone in an unhappy marriage abroad.

No doubt, David and I were very different in temperament, never mind the culture gap, but I think we did complement each other, managing a *yin–yang* balance between my optimistic outlook and his thoughtful, if somewhat negative, nature. Our one common defect was the fact that we both tended to bottle things up rather than talk them through openly and honestly. In the first eight years of our marriage, before Conall was born, we were very wrapped up in each other, to the exclusion of others – so much so that I did not have a confidant, nor even any close friends, until later in my life. As the relationship became increasingly distant and remote, I might not have been so lonely if I had had a sister or close girlfriend to satisfy my need for company. The marriage might have survived.

There were other pressures too, though. Working in journalism during the Troubles meant being on edge all the time and for many, including David, life was often a potent mix of long hours, stress and hard drinking. The cracks really began to show when David moved out of the marital bed when Owen was only a toddler, because of the snoring problem that had developed during my pregnancy. From then on we had separate bedrooms, even on holiday. Although there was the occasional physical contact, the intimacy of a married couple was gradually being eroded. My sense of rejection was compounded by resentment at the fact that the onus of making changes always seemed to fall on me.

External changes were also affecting our relationship. When

he returned to Northern Ireland after his two-year stint in Hong Kong, David rejoined the *Belfast Telegraph* as the local-government correspondent; then he became political correspondent, a position he held for fifteen years. He reported the news throughout a turbulent period in Northern Ireland's political history, from the hunger strikes to the Anglo-Irish Agreement, and was well respected by press officers and politicians. During an internal restructuring in the paper in the 1990s, he was moved temporarily to general news reporting. Understandably, he regarded this as a demotion and felt humiliated and aggrieved. Although he later became a sub-editor, writing some brilliant headlines and editing other reporters' stories, he missed not being on the frontline, where the action was.

Early on, when David was a well-known journalist in an important position, I was a nobody, a stranger from the other side of the world, with no local connection to anyone. Not yet fluent in English and unfamiliar with the systems and the culture, I was very reliant on David while I got to know the people and customs in my adoptive country. Whilst he was always supportive, and I always had great admiration for him, there was an inherent imbalance of power and the marriage partnership was not exactly equal.

Gradually, though, I became more confident and less dependent on David. After qualifying as a social worker, my career blossomed and I became wholly independent of him – not only emotionally but also financially. When I became the CWA director I even earned more than him – a fact that made him uncomfortable. He found it difficult to accept not being the main breadwinner any more. Perhaps in our generation, in those days, men tended to resent being overtaken by their wives. Moreover, I was gaining publicity and recognition as an ethnic-minority spokesperson in Northern Ireland. By his early fifties, as my career was going from strength to strength, his was winding down. This fundamental shift in our status gave rise to power struggles in making family decisions, big or small.

I always knew David loved me in his own understated way, although he had difficulty showing affection, and that he was proud of my achievements. However, in our later years together, I felt trapped in a relationship that was not only devoid of intimacy but also wrecked by constant point-scoring and bickering. My way of coping was to concentrate on building a career and a life for myself and our sons – but that, I think, only exacerbated his anxiety and withdrawal. Inevitably, we began to talk about a separation. Strangely, a couple of men made advances towards me around that time – which I flatly declined, as I detest cheating in relationships, but they made me realise I was still attractive to the opposite sex.

Despite two attempts at marriage counselling, things came to a head in 2001, when our sons were aged nineteen and sixteen. Conall was already away at university in England. We agreed to separate, ending our twenty-six-year marriage. It was as amicable as it could be under the circumstances and the boys accepted the breakup with amazing maturity and understanding. I bought a small semi-detached house in Holywood and moved there in the summer with Owen, who maintained regular weekly visits to his father in his new home in Knocknagoney, not far away. In spite of the family upheaval, Owen did very well in his GCSE examinations and went on to study for A levels at Sullivan.

Despite the unfortunate ending to our marriage, David and I had two absolutely wonderful sons, who did us both proud. We were particularly pleased that they were not only intelligent but also very socially conscientious and caring young men, each on a journey towards becoming valuable individuals and contributing to the world.

David and I actually got on much better after the divorce and I would consult him now and again on political matters. He always had helpful responses. Sadly, he died from a heart attack in mid-December 2010, a fortnight after his sixty-third birthday. He had retired in May of the previous year. His close colleague, Robin Morton, wrote in David's obituary, 'It is of some consolation to those of us who knew him and worked with him that he had spent several happy hours in the company of a group of former *Telegraph* colleagues at a Christmas lunch in Belfast earlier on the day he died.' He had gone after lunch to the Continental Market in front of the City Hall, where he had suffered the fatal heart attack. It was a comfort to us all that he had had an enjoyable day and that his death had been instant. Both our sons being in England, I went to the mortuary to identify him formally. He looked peaceful, as if he was asleep.

It was a bitterly cold winter and a fierce snowstorm was raging throughout the British Isles. Conall and Owen got stuck in Heathrow for hours the next day on their way back to Belfast. They were eventually diverted to Dublin Airport and arrived there at midnight. I was relieved that they had made it back to take care of their dad's wishes for his funeral and his estate. Stephanie, David's sister, was turned away at the airport when her flight was cancelled and, unfortunately, missed the funeral. However, she came over a week later and met with a number of David's former colleagues, who shared anecdotes about David with her. This gave her some solace.

Trudy, meanwhile, was devastated by David's premature death. He was the second of her children to die before her – Nicholas, who had suffered from schizophrenia for many years, had also died from a heart attack some years previously. As a mother, it must have been heartbreaking for her. Her health went downhill and she passed away peacefully in January 2012. Trudy had been a very loyal and active member of the Alliance Party for many years and a large number of party members, including David Ford, then party leader and justice minister, attended her funeral.

12

Into Politics, 2007

One morning in mid-December 2006, I had a visitor who called unexpectedly to my office and changed the course of my career and life irrevocably. It was the charismatic deputy leader of the Alliance Party, Naomi Long, whom I had known socially through my mother-in-law, Trudy, an active member of the east Belfast branch of the Alliance Party. However, more recently, Naomi and I had worked together on Belfast City Council's Good Relations panel, of which she was the chair.

Being the straight-talking, no-nonsense person she is, Naomi came directly to the point: 'Anna, we are looking for a candidate for South Belfast for the Assembly elections next March. Would you be interested?'

Although I had met many senior politicians – through my former husband, David, while working at the BBC and while lobbying for racial equality – I had never for one minute contemplated getting into government, particularly not the complex web of Northern Irish politics. I was very flattered to be asked, but it came as a big surprise. Naturally, I was hesitant about committing myself at a moment's notice. I asked Naomi, 'How long have I got to think about it?' Looking a bit sheepish, Naomi said, 'The deadline for candidate nomination in the party is 5 p.m. tomorrow. You have to be quick!'

I suspected I was not the first person they had approached during the process and wondered how many others had turned them down. Encouraged by the fact that I had not declined her proposal outright, Naomi brought along David Ford, the party leader, later on that afternoon to further persuade me. I promised to give it my serious consideration and let them know the following day.

Pleased, but obviously apprehensive at the prospect of becoming a candidate, I contacted David, who was then a sub-editor of the *Belfast Telegraph*, and a number of keen political observers I knew. The consensus was that as Alliance's Steve McBride had lost out to Carmel Hanna of the SDLP by only 151 votes in South Belfast in the 1998 Assembly election, it could be a winnable seat for Alliance in the next one. The constituency was also the most culturally diverse part of Northern Ireland, with a good mix of settled and new immigrants, who would be likely supporters of someone not from the traditional brand of orange or green politics.

I was not a member of any political party but we had always voted for Alliance in east Belfast. David and I were also admirers of the SDLP leader, John Hume, for his courageous role in the peace process. Coming from outside and not being a Christian, never mind a Protestant or a Catholic, I had never felt any particular affinity for any party from one side or the other of the political divide. If I were to join any party, the cross-community and non-sectarian Alliance Party would be the only political home I would feel comfortable with. I rang Naomi the next day to express my willingness to give it a go and hurriedly joined the party for candidate selection.

There was, at that time, a sense of optimism in the air that Northern Ireland was changing for the better – that politics would be less tribal and more focused on bread-and-butter issues. I wanted to be part of that change. The more I thought about it, the more strongly I felt that getting into government would be a good idea. That way I could effect change directly, rather than vying for politicians' attention from outside. I was curious, too, to test reaction to my candidature, knowing that there had never been a non-white politician in Northern Ireland. It would be a challenge to the electorate. Would they accept a candidate who was clearly not from one of the two major communities?

The Management Committee of the Chinese Welfare Association was apprehensive to learn that I was running for election for a particular political party, given the neutral stance generally adopted by the Chinese community. Many chose not to engage in politics so that they would not be seen to be taking sides. It took some persuasion to convince them, first of all, that Alliance was a non-sectarian party with cross-community support, and secondly that an ethnic-minority person in government would give black and minority-ethnic communities a voice. I was grateful that they not only bought into the idea in the end, but that the chair, Danny Wong, also wrote to all members of the Chinese Welfare Association and the Chinese Chamber of Commerce to encourage them to register to vote and to give me their support.

The large majority of Chinese residents in Northern Ireland had mostly ignored political elections until then, even if they were entitled to vote. The complexity of local politics was off-putting and none of the political parties had really engaged with the Chinese community. This made them feel not just unsure of who to vote for, but actually excluded from the democratic process.

When January came, there was a flurry of activity – having photos taken for publicity material, meeting South Belfast Alliance members and making myself familiar with Alliance policies. Alliance stalwart Gordon Kennedy became my campaign manager and mentor. As a complete novice in electioneering, with absolutely no idea what to expect, I was most grateful to have Gordon, who was wise, experienced and gentle, to guide me along the way.

From 8 January onwards we covered a large part of the constituency, from the Lisburn Road to Carryduff and everywhere in between, surveying and canvassing continuously for over eight weeks, most evenings after work and Saturdays, until the day before polling on 7 March. The evenings were cold, sometimes icy and dark. Walking up some long or uneven driveways and steep steps to doors could be hazardous and there were stumbles and falls. Nevertheless, party members, volunteers, past and present councillors such as Sara Duncan, Margaret Marshall and Tom Ekin pounded the streets with me in their thick winter anoraks, armed with leaflets, clipboards and enthusiasm.

I was told on my first evening out never to go into anyone's home and we would usually cover a street in pairs so that we could look out for each other. On one evening, when I was surveying a street with party activist Brice Dickson, I came to a house where an elderly woman lived. She made a great effort to come to the door, unlocking several bolts, and insisted that I went inside. It was such a cold night and, anyway, she wanted help with reading something she had got in the post. I stepped inside and stayed for as short a time as I could. When I emerged from the house I found a very concerned Brice looking around for me, thinking I had fallen into a hole – or worse.

Later on in the campaign, on the advice of the police, I did have to wear a personal alarm in the shape of a wristwatch while out canvassing. I called it my 'fashion accessory'. Soon after the announcement that I was the Alliance candidate running for elections in South Belfast, I got some negative responses by post and by telephone, as well as some racist comments on social media. Some questioned whether I should be representing anyone in Northern Ireland, where I was not a native – even though I had lived here longer than some of the younger candidates, who had not even been born when I arrived.

A representative from a women's group that was planning to provide English lessons for new immigrants telephoned me to invite me to join their classes. I am sure she was well intentioned, but I found her rather patronising. She said, 'Anna, until you can speak proper English, people aren't going to vote for you. You can come to our classes to improve your English.' Feeling rather stung, I went on the defensive: 'Well, none of my lecturers at university ever criticised my oral or written English. I have a master's degree and A-level English literature. What improvement can you offer me in your English classes for foreigners?'

The woman put the phone down. However, she did knock my self-confidence a bit. I wondered whether that was the public perception of my English-language skills.

Meanwhile, the racist comments on social media escalated. A far-right website posted disgraceful personal insults and published my picture along with pornographic photographs of east-Asian women, associating me with prostitution. It was appalling that these white supremacist men stereotyped Asian women as sex objects. Unfortunately, the PSNI did not seem to be able to prosecute anyone for these grossly offensive messages and images.

On the whole, though, my experience of the campaign trail was very positive. People were pleasant, welcoming and encouraging; many were complimentary about the contributions of the Chinese community and promised me their support. I was heartened by some who expressed their view that it was about time that an individual who was not from the main communities got elected. Feedback from the doorsteps made us feel more confident and made us dare to hope that all our efforts might bear fruit.

I really enjoyed knocking on doors and talking to people from all walks of life. In the Belvoir estate, I came across a rather large middle-aged man who opened the door in his string vest and open shirt. He looked at me and said, 'We only vote DUP!' But before he closed his door, he added, 'But good luck to you, love!' I thought that was so Northern Irish, so warm and sincere.

The weekend before polling, my younger son, Owen, then aged twenty-two and a trainee architect in London, came over to help with canvassing and really enjoyed it. Being a handsome and charming young man, he was a boon – so much so that two women coming out of the polling station on the election day told me that they had voted for me because my son had won them over.

On polling day, I went to meet the elderly Chinese residents in the Hung Ling Chinese sheltered-housing scheme in the Markets area, as agreed previously, to escort them to the local primary school to cast their votes. Some of them were in their seventies and eighties but had never voted in any political elections in their lives, either in Hong Kong or here in Northern Ireland. The excitement in the polling station was infectious; even the polling staff were smiling and giggling with them. I was proud to see them taking their ballot papers to the booths and exercising their right to vote.

Counting was on the next day, 8 March, in the King's Hall. I was a bit run down towards the end of the campaign and got the flu a couple of days before polling. I was running a fever and my muscles were aching. Having never been to a counting venue, I was not sure how warm the cavernous King's Hall would be, so on the morning of the counting I pulled out an old woollen jumper with a turtle neck to keep me warm. At lunchtime in the ladies' I noticed that I had put it on back to front, but I thought it looked fine and kept it that way. At least it would keep my chest and neck warm. It was only when I saw some of the photographs in the press the next day that I realised that the collar of the jumper had been standing up so high that it covered not only my neck but also part of my chin as well. On the day I got photographed most in my life, I had my jumper on the wrong way round.

The atmosphere in the King's Hall was electric – full of tension, excitement and anticipation. The local and national broadcast and print media were out in force there. The Assembly had been suspended for four and a half years and there was much attention on this new attempt at power-sharing, so there were even some foreign journalists. Candidates and party supporters jostled each other behind the barriers of the lines of counting tables to watch the black boxes full of ballot papers being opened one by one. As the papers tumbled out of each ballot box, officials sorted them into bundles. While they were doing that, we swiftly recorded the first-preference votes for each candidate on individual ballot papers on our tally sheets to get an early indication of the voting trend. It was quite tricky and it took a little while to get the knack of looking at the ballot papers back to front, from our position facing the officials, at the opposite side of the tables. Being petite like me did not help either – I had to crane my neck to see over the barrier separating us from the counting staff.

However, the bustle and excitement of the tallying turned into a long, long wait. There were rounds and rounds of eliminations and recounting. The election used the single-transferable-vote system, with a quota for election and surplus votes being distributed to the remaining candidates according to preferences expressed on the ballot paper. I found it amazing that we were still manually counting ballot papers – an electronic mechanism could save so much time and manpower.

When all the results were finally announced, Alliance had won seven seats, one more than in the last Assembly election in 2003, with an increase in the overall vote share. I was delighted to get

3,829 first-preference votes, just 506 short of the quota required to be elected on the first count. It took until the eighth count for me to become the third MLA elected in South Belfast. What pleased me most was that the votes went right across the constituency – from both Protestant and Catholic areas.

The media coverage was phenomenal. The local press, north and south of the border, declared that I was the first person from a minority-ethnic community to become an elected representative in Northern Ireland. The national media claimed that I was the first Chinese person elected to any parliament or devolved assembly in the UK. Then, it was reported, I had made history as the first ever China-born parliamentarian in Europe. This was even publicly endorsed and praised by the Chinese government.

Media stories about me spread literally worldwide, from Japan, China, Taiwan, Hong Kong, Russia and Australia through various European countries to the USA. I was in forty-four American newspapers, as far as the party's election guru, Ian Parsley, could ascertain. An Alliance Party member who was on holiday in the USA brought back a copy of the *Boston Globe* containing a feature about me for my scrapbook.

Not surprisingly, the Hong Kong media went into overdrive, with television interviews and features in both the Chinese and English newspapers. Paul Leighton, the deputy chief constable of the PSNI, was passing through Hong Kong and the commissioner of the Hong Kong Police gave him a copy of a local newspaper to bring back to me. My sister, Mary, also sent me lots of newspaper cuttings and emailed me with the message that our parents would have been very proud of my election success. An unexpected outcome of this worldwide exposure was that friends I had lost contact with began reconnecting with me, not only from Hong Kong but also from the USA, Canada and Australia, where many of them now live.

I was very pleased that my début in politics had sent out a positive message to the world. Northern Ireland had not only entered into a new era of power-sharing government but also, by electing me against all the odds, showed that people in Northern Ireland were willing to embrace diversity. It was evidence that we were not as bigoted as the outside world had, at times, made us out to be. Only a short time before, a *Guardian* journalist had labelled us 'the race-hate capital of Europe'.

13

The Northern Ireland Assembly, 2007–11

After all the excitement of the elections and the elation that the media attention had brought, I came back down to earth – to the reality that I had actually been elected as a Northern Ireland legislator. I agonised over the dilemma of whether it was wise to leave the thriving CWA as its director in order to embark on an uncertain future in the wobbly new Assembly. I was mindful, too, that we were close to getting planning permission for a brand new purpose-built community resource centre and in the middle of major internal-governance restructuring.

The secretary of state, Peter Hain, had set the date for devolution at 26 March and warned that Stormont must either work or be closed down. I kept my job in the CWA just in case. Although the deadline came and went, Stormont eventually opened for business on Tuesday, 8 May, when MLAs presented themselves one by one inside the grand Plenary Chamber, with its panelled walls and freshly cleaned blue carpets carrying the Assembly motif, to sign up for a designation as unionist, nationalist or 'other'. In my view this system really served to institutionalise sectarianism in the Assembly. In Northern Ireland, I had often been put into the 'other' category for ethnic identification. It struck me as odd that, even though I was now in the seat of government itself, I was still in the 'other' group. All Alliance members were categorised as 'other'.

It was strange to see that the DUP leader, Ian Paisley, after decades of saying 'Never, never, never!' and even of likening power-sharing with Sinn Féin to 'treason', had now agreed to be partners with them in government. Paisley and his arch-enemy, Gerry Adams, leader of Sinn Féin, would now be sitting across the chamber from each other. Stranger still, I watched the relationship of Ian Paisley and Martin McGuinness, the deputy first minister, develop into one so cordial that the two were dubbed the 'Chuckle Brothers'. Disappointingly, the more moderate parties, the UUP and the SDLP, had both had their worst election results in history. This gave rise to predictions that, with the dominance of the DUP and Sinn Féin, Northern Ireland's sectarian fault lines would become deeper than ever. Despite this, and despite media predictions of being squeezed by the bigger parties, the Alliance Party had managed to increase its share both of seats and votes.

Our first Alliance Party team meeting took place in David Ford's cramped office. His table had only six chairs; another had to be brought in to accommodate the expanded group of MLAs. David was beaming from ear to ear like a Cheshire Cat. The enhanced Alliance party was going to be allocated a new team meeting room.

David Ford, Naomi Long, Seán Neeson and Kieran McCarthy retained their seats, while there were three new faces around the table. Stephen Farry, the party's previous general secretary and a North Down councillor, had replaced Eileen Bell, who had been the party's deputy leader and the Assembly speaker; Trevor Lunn, a long-time Lisburn councillor, had replaced Seamus Close; and then there was me, the complete novice. I watched their animated analysis of recent gains and losses in the various parties, feeling rather green and somewhat lost.

Our seven MLAs formed the bulk of a United Community group of nine, which included the only member from the Green Party, Brian Wilson, and the independent Dr Kieran Deeny, who had been elected on a cross-community platform supporting the retention of Omagh Hospital. We acted as the unofficial opposition for three years in the Assembly, without any ministers in the Executive until the devolution of justice powers in 2010, when David Ford was appointed minister for justice. Taking that job was not an easy decision for Alliance, as some viewed it as a poisoned chalice.

David Ford, party director Gerry Lynch and I were invited to speak at the Liberal Democrat Conference in Brighton in September 2007. Our presentation was well received, with enthusiastic applause and a standing ovation from the audience. It was the first time I had attended a party conference and I was fascinated to recognise faces I had seen on national television for years. With Alliance being the Lib Dems' sister party, they were all very warm and supportive, making us feel very welcome. I met members of a Chinese Liberal Democrat group, who have maintained contact with me ever since.

As a parliamentary party of only seven, Alliance MLAs all

had multiple committee memberships. With my years in the community and voluntary sector, as well as my experience in higher education as a mature student, I was content that the party assigned me to the committees on Social Development, Employment and Learning, and Audit. The seven of us met on Monday mornings for a two-hour meeting to go over the business of the fortnight before the plenary session, which started at noon with prayer, when Assembly members stand in silence for two minutes. This was fine for me – not coming from any faith, I did not know any prayers. However, with each of us in our own room, holding different portfolios and being very busy, I found that very often, between team meetings, I did not have much contact with my colleagues.

The days flew past, filled with correspondence, events, meetings and phone calls. A lot of preparation was required before committee meetings, which involved reading a thick file of briefings, research papers and correspondence. The role of the committees is to scrutinise draft legislation and the performance of the various departments and their ministers. They also have the power to conduct inquiries and produce reports, some of which have been influential, with their recommendations acted upon. Committee membership is an important role and I hope I took it seriously. I was an active member of all three of my committees.

In scrutinising draft laws, committees engage with relevant stakeholders and department officials. Although in that first term the Assembly was often criticised for not bringing enough bills through, the committees I was on did consider a number of bills and statutory regulations, regarding housing, landlord registration, liquor licensing, charities – and, of course, the infamous Welfare Reform Bill. The Employment and Learning Committee produced a number of worthwhile reports – for example, on workplace disputes; young people not in education, employment or training (NEETs); and teacher training – which all had significant impact on policies and practices.

All the committees I was a member of in my first Assembly term collaborated well on a range of issues for the common good, without interference from divisive party politics. That, in my view, is where the committees are most effective. They bridge the gap between civil servants and communities through elected representatives on the ground.

Soon after the Assembly was re-established, the first and deputy first ministers hosted their first public engagement, with a reception in Parliament Buildings for civic society. They invited representatives from trade unions, churches and ethnic minorities. I was absolutely delighted by this gesture of inclusivity and the representatives from various ethnic communities not only enjoyed the evening but also hoped that there would be more opportunities for them to participate in government in future. So, on the first day of full business in the new term, I stood up to ask for a 'point of order', an opportunity to speak. MLAs looked at me, surprised.

I said:

On a point of order, Mr Speaker: is it in order for me to thank the First and Deputy First Ministers for the civic reception that they held in Stormont last Wednesday for ethnic-minority communities? I congratulate both ministers on a very successful event that sent out a strong message that the Assembly values the contributions of ethnic-minority communities and will not tolerate any form of racism against them.

The speaker smiled as he responded: 'That is not a point of order, but I have been very liberal in taking it. I am sure that the First and Deputy First Ministers have heard the Member's statement.'

I was therefore the first MLA, apart from the speaker, recorded in Hansard to speak in the new Assembly in May 2007. I was glad to put down an immediate marker declaring that politicians would not accept racism.

One of the first motions for debate was on gender equality in the Assembly and many new female MLAs used that moment for their first speech. I chose not to, even though I agreed with the idea that the Assembly lacked proportionate female representation. I thought it would be repetitive and predictable for all the women to advocate on that same subject. I later delivered my maiden speech on the subject of affordable housing. I thought it was important to show that female MLAs were not only there to highlight women's or family issues.

Alliance MLAs all had portfolios tied to committee memberships and usually spoke in the chamber on issues relevant to those remits. As small numbers of bills were going through, plenary sessions were filled by private members' motions for debate, which were quite often of no consequence. MLAs from bigger parties had more speaking rights and at times it was frustrating to sit in the chamber for ninety minutes during each debate, listening to the same facts and opinions being regurgitated again and again.

Apart from expressing opinions on topics relating to employment and learning and social development, I spoke on a number of other issues that were dear to my heart. I instigated a number of motions, adjournment debates and questions on funding cuts to the arts sector and community relations. I highlighted, for example, the annual cost of division in Northern Ireland, gender and race inequality, sexual crime and human trafficking. As a long-term advocate against human trafficking, I was glad to help launch the UK-wide Blue Blindfold anti-trafficking campaign in Northern Ireland and later set up the Assembly All-Party Group (APG) on Human Trafficking, which worked closely with similar parliamentary groups in the EU to share information on how best to tackle this horrible crime.

I also established the Assembly APGs on Ethnic Minorities and Sexual Health and was a member of a number of other such groups. The number of APGs had mushroomed to an almost unmanageable extent for busy MLAs, but it was still disappointing that, whilst outside ethnic-minority representatives were attending the APG on Ethnic Minorities in huge numbers and with great enthusiasm, the attendance of the politicians themselves was extremely poor. The chairpersonship was rotated between the political parties to encourage ownership and participation, but this did not work. Some MLAs privately expressed the view that, as they had few black and minority-ethnic residents in their constituency, racial equality was of no interest to them. This was disheartening – it was the same old argument that had been thrown at us when we had campaigned for the Race Relations Order over a decade before.

Apart from working in Parliament Buildings, all MLAs have their own constituency offices to handle enquiries from constituents. After the election, I looked around for suitable premises for my office. Following discussions with the party, which proposed some necessary structural renovation, I settled with setting up my office in the Alliance Party Headquarters on University Street. I rented two ground-floor offices for myself and my staff and shared all the facilities of the building. David Ford opened my office in an official launch the following February and I was delighted that many representatives from local residents' groups and networking organisations attended the event, entertained by a musical recital by the pupils of the nearby Botanic Primary School and a Chinese lion dance to bless the building.

Coming from a community-development background, I was very keen to form strong links with the local communities and set about attending meetings of local groups across the constituency, from the Markets to Finaghy and from Belvoir to Rosetta. I was a regular attendee at meetings of the newly formed Partners and Communities Together group in the Holylands, which aimed to deal with problems caused by houses of multiple occupancy and antisocial behaviour. It was gratifying to know that I could work in any of those areas and that people would be welcoming. I visited local schools belonging to both traditions and schools for children with learning disabilities; some invited me to speak at their assemblies and prize-giving ceremonies.

With the help of my very able constituency officer, Catherine Curran, who joined Belfast City Council in 2011, I dealt with an average of 300 constituency cases a year in the nine years to March 2016. These involved a broad range of issues including housing, planning, welfare benefits, health, education, employment, traffic and roads, discrimination, crime, paramilitary activity, sectarianism, racism and immigration. These were not cases with reference numbers; rather, they were vulnerable people facing social, financial, health and other problems who wanted our assistance.

Most of the time, the solution was simply a matter of writing a letter on behalf of a particular constituent to a particular public body. For example, one woman in her early sixties, who had developed arthritis in her hand and could no longer do her washing, got in touch with me. She wanted the Housing Executive to rearrange some cupboards in her tiny kitchen in order to make way for a washing machine, but was told she had to pay someone herself to do the renovation and plumbing. Living on her own and being on benefits, she was already struggling to be able to buy a washing machine. The expenses of the kitchen-adaptation work were out of her reach. We wrote to the Housing Executive, enclosing a letter from her GP. Fortunately, the Housing Executive then did the work without charging her.

With the reassessment of Disability Living Allowance claimants, we helped a number of constituents to appeal and, on occasion, worked with the Law Centre to represent them to tribunal stage. We were successful in enabling some of them to maintain their level of benefits.

I am proud to say that we gained our constituents' trust, as we always did our utmost to get the best outcome for them and to treat them with empathy. My experience in social work really stood me in good stead.

We had very appreciative constituents, too. Our offices in Stormont and South Belfast had hundreds of thank-you cards on the window sills and the walls. At Christmas we would get boxes and boxes of chocolates and biscuits. On one gloomy wintry day, a Chinese constituent brought me a delicious roast duck she had just cooked. The fragrant aroma wafted through the offices all day. Poor Catherine, a vegetarian, had to endure the smell of cooked meat for hours with no escape.

I also supported local campaigns to save the local post offices, regenerate the Village area, tackle flooding and deal with antisocial behaviour. With volunteers from the Business in the Community charity we helped to clear an area of no-man's land covered in almost knee-high grass between the railway line and the back of a row of terraced houses occupied mostly by elderly people. I found that rolling up your sleeves and mucking in was a most practical way of being accessible to constituents.

Soon, in May 2010, there was another polling day looming. This time eighteen MPs from Northern Ireland were to be elected to Westminster. The Alliance Party contested all eighteen seats and, although I stood in South Belfast, all our hopes and most of our efforts went towards Naomi Long in East Belfast. During the 2007 Assembly elections she had won just fifty-three votes fewer than Peter Robinson. We believed that Naomi could win the seat. It was a very rigorous and effective campaign. Members, staffers and volunteers pulled together to deliver leaflets and targeted letters and knocked on doors day and night during the months leading up to polling. People were amazed to open their doors to the justice minister, David Ford, urging them to support Naomi Long, with a police bodyguard standing at a discreet distance.

I was invited to a hustings in London, organised by a Chinese campaigning project to encourage Chinese young people to get into politics. The candidates, all first- or second-generation Chinese, all stood for the major parties in Britain – Conservative, Labour or Liberal Democrat. Coming from a party almost unknown in UK mainstream politics, I realised how marginalised Northern Ireland politics were in Westminster. I would be very much at sea if I were elected to Westminster.

On 6 May, Naomi won by a handsome margin in East Belfast. We were all jubilant that Alliance was on the rise, with our own wonderful deputy leader an MP. At the beginning of the election campaign, bookies' bets for her to win had been 100 to 1 and some staff had had the foresight to put a fiver on her winning. They all got a nice windfall after her victory. One member of staff in Alliance headquarters had bet £50 and won a handsome £5,000, to everyone's delight. Although we would lose her from local politics, we knew Naomi, articulate and hard working, would be very active in the House of Commons, representing her constituency most effectively as its member of parliament.

On reflection, over my first years in the Assembly, I found the majority of MLAs amicable. Ian Paisley, Martin McGuinness and Gerry Adams were always very cordial to me. Once, when answering a question from me in the chamber during Question Time, Ian Paisley said that he would take a leaf out of my book when it came to advocating for racial equality. He probably remembered first meeting me in the BBC when I was a young secretary. On one social occasion in the Long Gallery of Parliament Buildings before he stepped down as first minister, I said to him, 'Dr Paisley, people have asked me what my relationship with you is like. I told them that Dr Paisley has a soft spot for me because he knew me when I was a young bride!' Ian Paisley threw his head back and roared with laughter, while his wife, Eileen, nodded her head in agreement. Despite our differences in politics, I had always found the 'big man' and his wife very affable.

I had little direct contact with Peter Robinson. My first exchange with him outside of the debating chamber was when he chided me for putting too much soup into my bowl while he was queuing behind me in the basement canteen.

'Have you not got enough?' he asked. I probably had.

Strangely, too, I found some journalists suddenly changed the way they interacted with me on air or in front of the camera once I became a MLA. Previously, I had been a well-respected ethnic-minority spokesperson invited to give an interview; now, as a public representative, one of the loathed politicians who invariably wanted publicity, I was fair game for media scrutiny and aggressive questioning. I was taken aback on a couple of occasions before I realised I now needed to prepare extra-well before I turned up for an interview. However, thinking back, I was probably still too naïve and trusting of journalists, who naturally love to get a scoop

This picture was taken at the Farmweek office – I'd had my hair cut short after the disastrous perm.

My mother, Henry, me and Mary when they came to visit us in Belfast in 1980. This picture was taken in the garden of our house in Holland Gardens.

1983, with David, Trudy and Conall at the cottage in the Mournes where we spent so many happy weekends and holidays.

Outside the cottage with David and the boys.

A Lo family photo in Hong Kong, 1987. Front row (L–R): Lulu, Edith, Owen, my mother, Conall and Lisa. Back row (L–R): me, Raymond, my three brothers, my brother-in-law and Mary.

At Buckingham Palace, receiving my MBE in 2000, with Conall, David and Henry.

At Conall's graduation in Nottingham.

At Owen's graduation at the University of Italian Switzerland.

With Catherine Curran and Kate Nicholl.

Conall and Fiona's wedding in Oxford, 2016.

Henry ringing to congratulate me on my election win in 2007.

Casting my vote in the European election in May 2014 at Cooke Centenary Church in Belfast.

for their programme or newspaper, regardless of the potential consequences for a politician.

Soon after becoming a public figure, I received threats of arson on my home. The Northern Ireland Office provided some security measures around the house and I was advised, yet again, to carry a personal alarm, as well as to check under my car every day. I joked with the crime-prevention officer that getting on my knees on my drive to look under my car every morning before going to work would ruin all my tights. But I suppose it was not a laughing matter. The PSNI also put me on 'rapid response', so that if I ever made an emergency call the police would be at my house quickly. For a while a police patrol car cruised daily around the development I lived in. Little did I know that this would become a regular occurrence over the next few years, wherever I moved. The neighbours seemed to catch on very quickly. When they suddenly saw a police vehicle driving up and down their street, they knew a politician had moved in amongst them.

I won some recognition, too, and received a number of awards, which included an award from the UK-wide 48 Group Club for promoting trade between Northern Ireland and China and *Irish Tatler* magazine's Woman of the Year Northern Ireland Award for 2009. It was pleasing to receive these accolades and I treasure the memory of the pomp and ceremony of the presentations in the Chinese Embassy in London and at a glamorous gala dinner in Dublin.

14

Getting Re-elected, 2011

Encouraged by Naomi Long's resounding success in the Westminster elections, we forged ahead with increased confidence for the Northern Ireland Assembly and local-council elections, to be held on the same day in May 2011. The Alliance Party already had a strong team of councillors in Belfast City Council and Catherine Curran, who had been my constituency officer for four years, stood as a new candidate in the Laganbank district for the first time. She had worked very hard for constituents and was therefore very popular in the area.

The Assembly had been seen as slow to make progress in the previous term, although people seemed to accept that the mandatory coalition of five parties of very different ideologies and policies needed time to bed in and learn to work together. However, it was expected that the Assembly would deliver much more in its second term.

No one could risk taking the electorate for granted, so we went out in force again in my constituency of South Belfast, knocking on doors and engaging with residents. With a May election, the weather was much kinder to us this time. Catherine and I went out together often, doing surveys in the various neighbourhoods. I remember meeting one constituent and, when I urged her to vote for Catherine, she replied with a laugh, 'Don't worry, Anna! All the residents in this street will be giving her their vote!' They were rewarding her for her help in blocking an unwanted development behind their street.

Polling day came and went, with counting on 6 May, again in the King's Hall. Very early on in the count we knew that both Catherine and I were doing well, and again I was really pleased to see votes for me coming out of ballot boxes from right across the constituency. In the first count, I topped the poll with 6,390 votes, almost doubling my first-preference total at the last election. I was over the moon. Being the single Alliance candidate had made life easier for me, of course, since votes were not split between party colleagues. I watched some candidates from the DUP, the SDLP and the UUP struggling with anxiety, which was showing on their faces, waiting to know their fate as count after count went on into the night. We were delighted for Catherine, too, who topped the poll in Laganbank. Winning such overwhelming support when standing for the first time is rare. It was a testimony to her hard work in the constituency office.

Although media commentary reported that the results largely kept the status quo, with few new faces, we were happy. Not only had we retained all our existing Assembly seats, but we had also gained one in East Belfast and increased the number of Alliance local councillors. It was good to see Judith Cochrane, a Castlereagh councillor and constituency worker for Naomi Long, get elected as the second MLA in East Belfast.

With eight MLAs, the Alliance Party was now entitled to a ministerial position and the chairmanship of a committee. Stephen Farry became the minister for employment and learning and, in my view, was one of the most effective ministers in the second Assembly term. David Ford, able and hard working, continued to tackle successfully the many challenges in his difficult role as minister for justice. I have great admiration for them both, in their intellect and their vision for a shared future.

As for me, I was chuffed to bits to be appointed chairperson of the Environment Committee. Having been born and brought up in a concrete jungle, I had fallen in love with the natural beauty of the countryside in Northern Ireland as soon as I arrived in the mid-seventies. As a family, we had spent a great deal of time roaming the rural areas of County Down when the children were growing up and we have always appreciated the natural environment and the need to protect our wildlife and natural heritage, now and in the future. Conall, from his late teens into his university days, was a fervent advocate of carbon reduction and I was much influenced by him as a member of a younger generation more attuned to the need for environmental sustainability. On completion of his pharmacy degree at Nottingham University, Conall won a UK-wide competition as graduate of the year for promoting environmental awareness on campus, with a handsome cash prize and a wonderful glass shield, which he gave me to keep. The shield has pride of place in my home.

That June I went for the first time to the Northern Ireland Environment Link Conference. I bragged as a proud mother about Conall winning the accolade, but confessed in modesty, too,

'I am passionate about the environment but I don't know enough. However, I am all ears, ready to learn from you, the experts in the field.'

The Environment Committee was supported ably by a very competent secretariat, headed by the committee clerk, Alex McGarel, who has a PhD in botanical science and years of experience in the committee. Alex was a resourceful mine of information. I went out and about in earnest in the early summer, meeting environmental groups and visiting projects of the Mourne Heritage Trust. I had a boat trip on Strangford Lough organised by Ulster Wildlife, to view first hand the damage to the horse mussels on the sea bed. I was in my element – outside and learning. In June, I was thrilled to sponsor the RSPB's Marine Task Force walk to Stormont. The schoolchildren who took part brought with them a model of a basking shark, made to highlight the need for a marine bill. It was delightful to watch the children carrying the model up the hill in brilliant sunshine. Some had dressed up and had their faces painted as sea creatures. I firmly believe that, if we educate our young people about the environment, they will carry the torch into the future and value our natural resources the way they should be valued.

Days after the May election, I was privileged to be invited to a lunch hosted by the Irish president, Mary McAleese, in Áras an Uachtaráin in the Phoenix Park, for Queen Elizabeth's historic visit to Ireland. It was the first event of the queen's four-day state visit. I was surprised to find that it was quite a small gathering – just a few tables with people from diplomatic circles, several politicians and VIPs from both the north and south of Ireland.

John and Pat Hume were there, but I was especially delighted to meet the charming Barry Douglas, our renowned pianist, whom I had seen perform on stage previously.

It was not the first time I had had the great honour of meeting the two heads of state. President McAleese was a frequent visitor to Northern Ireland and I was always very impressed by her great intellect and accessibility. I had met Queen Elizabeth for the first time in 2000, when she had awarded me the MBE in Buckingham Palace. David, Conall and Henry had come to the ceremony with me, but Owen had been away in Switzerland, camping with the scouts. Owen still laughs at me for not recognising the famous footballer Ian Wright. Ian Wright had chatted to me in a reception area for the recipients waiting to get their awards and I, ignorant of the football scene, asked him if he was a community worker like me. I tend to put my foot in it sometimes. However, in my defence, I had been in awe in that gallery area, admiring the priceless masterpieces on the walls.

I had been invited to Hillsborough Castle twice again after that to meet the queen. I attended a private lunch for her and Prince Philip, at which she met about twenty representatives from different sectors in Northern Ireland. On another occasion, I was chosen, amongst others, to greet the couple at a garden party in the magnificent surroundings of Hillsborough. It was a pleasure to meet Queen Elizabeth, who is always gracious and diplomatic.

Unfortunately, life for me was not often plain sailing. Whilst I was still rejoicing in my second election success and absolutely delighted at having the new responsibility of the Environment Committee chair, my home life was falling apart.

15

Second Divorce

After separating from my husband David Watson in 2001, I met Gavin, a divorcé, within a couple of months. I was really on the rebound at that time, longing for love and attention. Gavin, five years younger than me at forty-six, had been a fire officer in Belfast during the 1970s and had witnessed some of the worst atrocities of the Troubles. He was a sales manager when we met. Loving, attentive and affectionate, he was almost the opposite of David and I soon found myself in love again.

We bought a house together the following spring – too soon, really – in picturesque Islandmagee, although my younger son, Owen, and I continued to live in my house in Holywood for another year, until Owen finished his schooling at Sullivan Upper School. Gavin was delighted that his eight-year-old son from a previous relationship was then able to move in with him. Owen and I went over to Islandmagee at weekends and during school holidays. Gavin thought the world of my two sons and they, in turn, were amicable with him. Gavin's son looked up to Owen, the clever big brother he never had.

Initially we were happy, but I soon discovered that some of the things Gavin had said about himself were untrue. He told me, for example, that the Fire Service had sponsored him to go to Oxford University to complete a part-time degree, and that his family had a share in the farm on which he had been renting a cottage. It was only after we had bought the house and after the funeral of his father, when I spoke to a close relative of his, that I found out the truth about his academic and employment backgrounds. More importantly, though, I heard that he had a history of bullying and that allegations of domestic violence towards previous partners had been made against him.

I challenged him about this, but he denied lying to me. I understood that he had been trying to impress me when we had first met by telling me all those half-truths, and that they had probably originated from a sense of inadequacy. I made it clear that the past was the past, but that from that point on there must be honesty and integrity in our relationship. As for the allegations of domestic violence, he also vigorously denied those. I didn't know what to believe but I wanted to give him the benefit of the doubt. However, after a while – particularly after Owen left for Cambridge University and I moved in with him full time – I began to see occasional displays of temper, erratic driving and bullying behaviour.

Gavin was supportive of my work in the CWA and later on, when I went into politics. We spent lots of quality time together, with a busy social calendar and fabulous holidays abroad, which I had never had before. He was well travelled from his worldwide motor-rally and naval-reserve trips, including tours to Iraq and the Falkland Islands. He was often in his element when we attended events and always sociable, but admitted being jealous at times when people paid me a lot of attention as the invited politician.

We moved to a beautiful home in Jordanstown in 2005. However, in late 2007 he began to take medication for a health issue and his behavioural problems became worse. I had a very difficult time coping with his worsening temper tantrums, road rage and irrational behaviour, which had even started to occur in public. That Christmas, driving home from an event to which he had insisted on accompanying me, he became very angry. The event had finished late and he had missed a favourite television programme. When he stopped at a set of traffic lights, I jumped out of the car, telling him that I would take a taxi home because he was driving dangerously. But he caught up with me, dragged me back to the car, got in beside me and hit me in the stomach. I was winded. When I got my breath back, I foolishly told him to drive to the police station so that I could report the incident.

'You are not going to get away with this!' I sobbed. However, I quickly realised that he was in such a rage that arguing with him further would be likely to cause a serious car accident and probably get us both killed.

I was concerned for him, but increasingly felt vulnerable and unhappy.

In July 2008, just two days before we left for a campsite in France for a holiday, we found out from the news on the radio that the drug he had been taking could cause serious mental-health side effects – even suicides. He immediately came off it and was understandably very angry about being given it in the first place. But we had a nightmare of a holiday. On one occasion towards the end of the dreadful fortnight, after a humiliating evening of temper tantrums in one restaurant after another (the restaurant owner had to drive me back to the campsite after Gavin had stormed out), I told him I had had enough and had decided to leave him. He then locked the caravan door and threatened that he might cut his wrists.

As soon as we arrived back in England I did leave, bundling a change of clothing and some toiletries into a plastic bag and walking out while he was having a shower. I took a train to London to stay with Owen who was soon to attend his master's degree course in the Academy of Architecture in the University of Italian Switzerland. I was traumatised and completely heartbroken.

On my return to Northern Ireland, I rented a flat in South Belfast while Gavin stayed on in Jordanstown. His son, then fifteen, left that August to live with his mother abroad. Gavin, meanwhile, proactively sought therapy, supposedly at times in a military hospital in England, claiming that he was determined to get better and win me back.

I went back to him after nine months' separation, believing that the treatment had improved his behaviour. I now believe, though, that his volatility was more an innate problem than a condition brought on by the medication. Anyhow, I eventually agreed to marry him and we wed, amongst friends and relatives, in a humanist ceremony in July 2010 in the majestic setting of the Great Hall at Stormont. The ceremony included a spectacular lion dance and traditional Irish and Chinese music.

Sadly, the jubilance and happiness engendered by the unique wedding did not last for long. In August 2011, after we had been married for thirteen months, we got into an argument inside our motor-home, which was parked beside the house. Gavin struck me on both sides of my face. I was stunned into silence. I got out of the parked vehicle and went into the house. Gavin followed and pushed me from behind. I fell flat on the floor in the hall. In tears, I got up and asked: 'Why did you do that?'

'You provoked me,' he responded. 'You deserved it.'

Later, however, he broke down in tears and apologised.

A few days later I developed severe whiplash from the force of the push. The neck injury caused me excruciating pain and stiffness for over six weeks, and its effects lasted for more than two years. On one visit to my GP the pain was so bad that I had to have X-rays to make sure that I had not actually cracked a bone. Luckily, although the X-rays showed only signs of wear and tear, my neck was intact. I needed daily neck exercises and took up swimming again to strengthen my neck muscles.

I went back to work in mid-September when the Assembly reopened after the summer recess. I was still struggling with the pain but what bothered me more was the fact that I had to lie to cover up the real cause of the injury. I warned Gavin in no uncertain terms that, if anything like that ever happened again, I would leave him for good.

Sadly, another episode did happen, a few months later in November 2011. After a social event one Friday evening, he got something in his eye and we went to a hospital emergency department to get it checked out. Although nothing was detected, he still complained of pain over the next two days. On the Sunday night, when I got into bed with a book, he became very annoyed that I had woken him and began to shout at me. He snatched the book from my hand and threw it across the room. I made to get out of bed and go to the spare bedroom but he restrained me. I was frightened that he was going to head-butt me and shouted, 'I'm calling the police'. He then let go of me and got out of bed, picking up the book and throwing it at me. It hit me on the hip.

I hardly slept that night, consumed by searing anger. It dawned on me that his pattern of abusive behaviour meant that I was never going to feel safe with him. I realised that things were unlikely to change, despite therapies and promises. I came to the clear realisation – a light-bulb moment, really – that my home was not a sanctuary, but rather an unsafe place that could cause serious harm to my physical health and mental wellbeing. I knew there would always be excuses for unacceptable behaviour. Exhausted and heartbroken once again, I packed a suitcase, wrote him a letter and left for good the next morning.

I could have demanded that Gavin move out of our luxury home in Jordanstown, as I owned most of it, but it seemed much easier at the time for me to leave. In order to make sure he would not have to suffer financial hardship and would still be able to make the mortgage payments, I left all the money in our bank accounts for him. In hindsight, this was a mistake. It made it too easy for him to stay on, and helped lead to the subsequent years-long struggle between us over selling the house.

He was persistent in wanting reconciliation but, whenever it did not go his way, he made verbal threats against me. After he had made one such threat over the phone in December, shortly after I left him, I contacted the police and made a statement about that and the incidents of assault. However, I did not wish to press charges for fear of reprisals from him and – given my position as a public figure – media intrusion if the matter proceeded to court. Sometimes I regret this. Bringing him to court would have highlighted the endemic problem of domestic violence – which can happen to anyone, from any background. It is vital for a victim to seek advice and help when he or she experiences domestic abuse in order to stop further occurrences and escalation of violence.

I have always been aware of the fact that ethnic-minority women are much more vulnerable to domestic violence than others. When I confided my experience to a friend from an ethnic-minority background, I was shocked to hear that she too suffered domestic violence in silence – her culture would not tolerate divorce. Moreover, many non-EU immigrants depend on their spouse's work status to live in the UK. If they divorce, they put their legal status at risk. For those with little English, it is also difficult to seek information about where to get help. Family support is vital at such times and many people just do not have their family around to encourage and help them to leave an abusive relationship.

I was granted a divorce, uncontested, on grounds of unreasonable behaviour. However, the emotional blackmail and bitter wrangling over the sale of the house and the eventual financial settlement, which lasted for years afterwards, were frustrating, distressing and draining. I could see myself ageing in front of my own eyes during this most difficult period in my life. I had made a grave error of judgement in going back to Gavin and marrying him, and paid heavily – emotionally, physically and financially – for the mistake.

After the separation, an old friend told me that she had never understood what I saw in Gavin. The truth was that after leaving David, whose mental health issues had made him distant from me, I was vulnerable to anyone showing me any affection. I had been lonely for so long that I longed for a chance to share my life again with someone loving.

Despite the turmoil and upheaval in my domestic circumstances, my political life went on, which no doubt helped me to keep my sanity during those extremely troubled years. I was grateful, too, for the support from my family, close friends and my loyal staff, Catherine Curran and Kate Nicholl.

16

Chairing the Environment Committee

It was a huge privilege and the highlight of my political career to chair the Environment Committee. I treasured the time I spent considering the many aspects of the extensive range of duties of the Department of the Environment (DoE), from environmental protection to planning, waste management and road safety. Over the five years, the committee scrutinised a number of new pieces of legislation and regulation, including marine environment, planning policies, local-government reform, carrier-bag levies, the alcohol limit for drink-driving offences, new drivers and taxi operations. The details of many of these issues were unfamiliar to me and I was really thrown in at the deep end, and had to learn fast.

However, I am very proud to have successfully amended the Marine Bill, the first bill that passed through the committee, inserting a new clause on 'sustainable development' at the very beginning of the act. It was a suggestion called for by the voluntary sector but rejected by departmental officials and other parties on the committee. To be truthful, I did not hold much hope that my amendment was going to receive enough support in the consideration stage in the chamber – but, to my astonishment and delight, I convinced them by saying that without sustainable development 'the bill has no soul'. The amendment thereby ensured that 'the Department must in exercising its functions under this Act – act in the way it considers best calculated to contribute to the achievement of sustainable development in Northern Ireland'.

After the debate, I left the chamber with Simon Hamilton beside me and told him that I was so happy I could have kissed him. My comments were later repeated in the further consideration and final stages, with Simon saying, 'I note that the Chair said she "could" have kissed me. As passionate as she was about marine management protection and looking after the marine environment, it was only "could" have kissed: she was not sufficiently motivated to actually do it. Even she could not go that far.' There were certainly some light moments in the chamber now and again.

The committee normally met weekly on Thursday mornings for about three hours in the grand setting of the Senate Chamber, with the session broadcast live to the public. Occasionally some informal meetings were held in smaller committee rooms. The acoustics in the Senate Chamber were initially very poor, making it quite difficult at times for me to hear witnesses who were softly spoken giving evidence at the other end of the massive table, which was also quite high. The red leather chairs were old and many of them had sunken seats. I had to reserve a chair with stiffer padding so that witnesses and the camera could see me sitting upright.

The chairperson has a lot of preparation to do before meetings.

I would have a briefing from the clerk and assistant clerk on Wednesday afternoons and would read papers afterwards for a couple of hours at home in the evening. Later on in the term, we changed to using an electronic device rather than a thick file of hundreds of pages of paper, which was certainly much more environmentally friendly. The committee staff I had the privilege of working with were all intelligent, diligent and professional, and we politicians really depended on their expertise for guidance.

Likewise, I found the departmental officials very amenable. We worked in genial partnership with them and those good working relationships were conducive to useful dialogue and progress. The result was that the minister and the department accepted most committee suggestions to improve draft legislation without much resistance. There were some prolonged exchanges between officials and the committee, but most of the time difficulties were ironed out and resolved by compromise.

I adopted a fairly informal and friendly approach in chairing these weekly meetings, addressing members and officials on first-name terms, even though it was a statutory committee with legislative power and the proceedings were formal. After my retirement I met a senior official from the DoE, who was very complimentary, saying that his staff had always been very willing to come before the committee because the atmosphere had been so positive and relaxed. As a representative of the smallest party in the Executive and the lone member from Alliance (DUP had four members, Sinn Féin three, SDLP two and the UUP one), I was in the minority and at a disadvantage. But I must say, on the whole, everyone gave me my place as the chair.

Alex Attwood of the SDLP was the environment minister at the time and he and I crossed swords several times. After I challenged him publicly on the proposed extra economic weight given to planning applications in the ill-fated Planning Bill, we both found ourselves at the launch of a publication on the history and archaeology of Dunluce Castle. It was a stormy day and I drove up the Antrim coast with Kate, my able research assistant, to the hotel where the launch was to take place. We were convinced that Alex Attwood was trying to ignore me, turning his back to me most of the time, but we managed to corner him eventually. A photographer was nearby and took a photograph of him and me together holding a copy of the book, smiling.

However, the Planning Bill was made worse in June 2013 by amendments from the DUP and Sinn Féin that gave OFMDFM powers over some planning-zone areas. That idea was then abandoned altogether after consideration stage, a decision of Attwood's that I fully supported. We clashed again when he granted planning permission for a proposed golf-hotel development in Runkerry, home to many wildlife species and just a mile from the Giant's Causeway, Northern Ireland's only UNESCO World Heritage Site and top tourist destination. On that occasion he rang me on my mobile when we were both on our summer holidays in different parts of Europe and spoke for quite some time about the fact that he was 'fuming' about comments I had made publicly. I suppose we were both trying to do our job to the best of our ability.

Mark H. Durkan was a very different environment minister from Attwood. He was witty and had been thrown in at the deep end, which made it difficult to be too hard on him. However, I did get very cross with him and the department's permanent secretary, Leo O'Reilly, about the mismanagement of funding cuts to NGOs in the environment sector in the spring of 2015.

With the Conservative government stepping up its austerity drive, Northern Ireland's public spending was further reduced in 2015–16, with DoE handed the largest percentage cut in its budget. On Thursday, 24 March 2015, the Environment Committee went to visit a recycling plant in County Meath. On crossing the border back up to Northern Ireland, my mobile started to alert me to a large number of emails from environmental NGOs, which had just received letters with devastating news of unprecedented funding cuts. DoE was slashing its Natural Heritage Grants programme to the sector, putting it into a serious crisis, with 130 potential compulsory redundancies and some organisations forced to close their doors within days.

I was alarmed, even though we all had expected that some cuts were inevitable, but the drastic nature of the decision was, in my opinion, utterly short-sighted. Many of these organisations had been set up by the Northern Ireland Environment Agency to manage designated areas, without which our capacity to protect the environment and meet government targets and EU obligations would be much reduced; without them, we would run the risk of huge EU infraction fines. Furthermore, the sector was value for money, as many environmental NGOs could leverage additional funds from UK and EU programmes as well as making use of a large workforce of volunteers.

I knew we had to act fast. During the one-and-a-half-hour

journey in the minibus travelling from Newry to Stormont that Thursday afternoon, we secured an emergency meeting with the minister the following Monday, as well as a pre-meeting briefing with representatives of the sector.

Mark H. Durkan and his senior staff attended the meeting, with dozens of NGO representatives sitting in the public gallery in the Senate Chamber. Committee members were forceful in questioning the minister on his budgeting. Durkan admitted that 'the cut to my Department is actually being placed on the shoulders of a small percentage of my budget, and that is where the NGOs are'. However, the minister accepted the criticism that the process had been badly managed and twice apologised to the sector, stating his regret about any damage that might have been caused to his relationship with organisations. More importantly, he committed to engage with the sector 'as a matter of urgency'.

I was glad and relieved for the sector when the minister announced in April that he would allocate some of the revenue gathered from the carrier-bag levy to fund environmental projects, thus reinstating most of money the cuts had removed. Happily, this stabilised the sector.

If that had not happened, we would not have had the first ever Environment Week in Northern Ireland in September 2015, which I initiated. The committee hosted events in Stormont in partnership with Northern Ireland Environment Link to celebrate our natural and built environment and to encourage everyone to play their part in preserving, protecting and cherishing it. The reception, workshops and seminars provided opportunities for environmental NGOs to engage with MLAs who were supportive of the events. We also introduced an initiative whereby individual MLAs would be species champions for a year, an innovative idea that we borrowed from the Scottish Parliament. Each species champion would have to promote a chosen species, occurring in their constituency, which was rare or facing difficulty in its natural habitat. Committee members enthusiastically became champions for barn owls, red squirrels, butterflies and so on. I was the champion for swifts and promised to put up nesting boxes in South Belfast in the spring. We have seen a decline of swifts coming to Northern Ireland, as many of our buildings are modern, lacking the nooks and crannies that these birds tend to nest in.

I sincerely hope that Environment Week was not a one-off event and that, given its success the first time round, the Assembly will make it not only an annual event but one that gets bigger and better each time.

On reflection, it was a real privilege to chair the Environment Committee for five years. I learned so much about the whole range of department issues. I never would have thought I could be so excited at the thought of visiting waste-management sites and exploring the concept of zero waste and the circular economy. It was wonderful, too, to develop a really good relationship with environmental NGOs – so much so that after retirement I joined the board of Keep Northern Ireland Beautiful as a volunteer.

It was a pity, though, that proposals for a national park, a climate-change bill and an independent environment-protection agency did not get enough political support and never materialised; but I am sure we will get there one day, hopefully not too far in the future.

17

The Goings-on in the Standards and Privileges Committee

Following a mid-term reshuffle in the team of Alliance MLAs, I took on two more committees: the Employment and Learning Committee and the Standards and Privileges Committee. In the latter I replaced Kieran McCarthy as deputy chair in October 2013. The Standards and Privileges Committee considers matters relating to the conduct of Assembly members, including reports from the Assembly's Commissioner for Standards on investigations into complaints that a breach of the code of conduct has occurred. I was assured by my party leader that the Standards and Privileges Committee only met occasionally and that the workload would be light. In the event, that was far from the case.

Unlike the other Assembly committees I had experience of, the Standards and Privileges Committee was often influenced by party politics when it came to dealing with complaints against MLAs – and, with three forthcoming elections, the political climate was inevitably heating up. People may say that that is politics, but I believed that this committee above all others should rise above party politics, with its members setting the good example of being impartial and respectful to each other. After all, members were not there to defend party interest, but to uphold the expected code of conduct of all MLAs, irrespective of which party they came from. Perhaps I was still politically naïve and too much of an idealist.

The membership of the committee – 4 from the DUP (including the chair), 3 from Sinn Féin and 1 each from the UUP, the SDLP, Alliance and the Green Party – favoured the two largest parties. The majority of complaints involved DUP MLAs. Strangely, Sinn Féin committee members seemed in general fairly lenient towards complaints against the DUP. When the DUP and Sinn Féin clubbed together, there was no way the smaller parties would win on any division. Perhaps it was a matter of scratching each other's backs.

When I joined the committee, Alastair Ross, the chairperson, was leading a review of the code of conduct for MLAs. Ross was one of the new generation of DUP members who were deemed better educated and more modern in their outlook than some of the old guard, who had come from the ranks of local councillors during the bad old days of the Troubles, when few people had wanted to become involved in local politics.

Soon the long-awaited controversial report on the Robinson affairs landed on the desk of the committee clerk. Shortly after a BBC *Spotlight* programme containing a number of allegations against Iris and Peter Robinson was broadcast on 7 January 2010, the Standards and Privileges Committee decided to ask Tom Frawley, then the interim Assembly Commissioner for Standards, to conduct an investigation. After various delays caused by the police investigation, a change of commissioner and the unavailability for interview of Iris Robinson, the new commissioner, Douglas Bain, finally produced a draft report in November 2013. This was promptly challenged by Iris Robinson's solicitor. Bain withdrew the draft report in February 2014 and produced a second draft report in March, which was withdrawn in May, again owing to objections from Iris Robinson's solicitor. Douglas Bain sent his third and final report to the committee on 3 July 2014.

I remember watching the BBC *Spotlight* programme in utter dismay. The allegations were the stuff of a Hollywood movie, involving high political life, corruption and sex. I was in the chamber while Peter Robinson answered questions, showing no sign of any distress, despite the fact that his wife had just attempted suicide. Most of us thought no political leader could come out of such a scandal unscathed. Miraculously, though, Peter Robinson survived the political hurricane when the party closed ranks in support of him.

After the summer recess, members were given the opportunity to read the report in a designated room but, in order to maintain confidentiality prior to the committee's formal consideration from 10 September 2014, were not allowed to take their copy out of that room. A couple of times journalists asked me when the report was likely to be published, but I kept my silence on its content. However, it was not long before certain details were leaked to the media.

The commissioner had cleared Peter Robinson of any wrongdoing but found that Iris Robinson had committed a serious breach of the code of conduct by failing to register her interest in three payments relating to loans from two developers. These loans were used by her lover, Kirk McCambley, to set up a business at the Lock Keeper's Inn in my constituency of South Belfast. It was quite a popular café, where many families or dog-walkers would go for a coffee and a rest after walking on the towpath; I had visited it often myself. I remember going in once after the BBC revelations and finding some customers gawking at McCambley, who had his head down and was busying himself behind the counter. I felt very sorry for him.

There was not much disagreement with the commissioner's conclusion in the committee. As usual, he had redacted some confidential and personal information contained in the report but, following consideration of correspondence from Iris Robinson's solicitor, the committee sought Assembly legal advice and made a large number of its own redactions as well.

Whilst I would always, of course, wish to comply fully with human-rights obligations, I felt that the committee was being over-cautious, if not overprotective of Iris and Peter Robinson in redacting such a large amount of information. I felt there was a certain unspoken pressure on various members of the committee, whose largest group seemed to want to delete as much detail as possible so as to limit damage to the DUP's reputation. It was indicated repeatedly that negative reporting could harm Iris Robinson's mental health, or worse, so there was a sense, too, that not to agree to redact the report would be callous.

The report was finally published on 28 November 2014, almost five years after the *Spotlight* programme was broadcast. I issued a press statement to welcome its publication, but also expressed my concerns about its delay. Furthermore, I stated that the deletion of so much of the content by the DUP-dominated committee did not do justice to the commissioner's original findings. The next day, when Robin Newton, a DUP committee member, passed me on the corridor, he challenged me about what I had meant by 'the DUP-dominated S. and P. Committee'. Protesting that the DUP's majority on the committee was entirely justified by their electoral mandate, he said, 'That's the workings of D'Hondt.'

I knew I would not be flavour of the month with the DUP, but I did not realise that the worst was yet to come. The DUP's Jimmy Spratt, whom I had known for years as a fellow South Belfast MLA, took over from Alastair Ross as chair of the Standards and Privileges Committee in January 2015. During the seven or eight meetings that took place between January and June, I felt that Spratt was rude and abrupt to members not from his own party. Sandra Overend from the UUP, Steven Agnew from the Green Party and I discussed among ourselves on more than one occasion what we viewed as bullying behaviour on Spratt's part. One member told me that he rolled his eyes whenever I spoke. I certainly got the impression that, whenever I raised my hand to request the right to speak, he looked displeased. On two occasions I found him dismissive of my requests for further information from the commissioner and the committee clerk. In fact, when I persisted, he accused me of challenging his authority as chair.

However, it was not only his manner towards me and others that I found unacceptable. It was his sniping, negative comments against the commissioner, made in closed sessions, with which I felt particularly uncomfortable. He also sought to steer the committee to submit an amendment to the Public Services Ombudsperson Bill to allow the new ombudsman to investigate any alleged maladministration in the office of the Standards Commissioner. Although this came to nothing, the proposed change would have eroded the commissioner's independence, which was guaranteed by law. The commissioner had previously conducted two investigations into complaints against Spratt, and Spratt had said on several occasions that this had been a negative experience. It raises the question of why the DUP wished to appoint him chair of this particular committee.

The commissioner reported to the committee on 18 March 2015 that he found that the DUP's Sammy Wilson had breached the code of conduct by calling Traditional Unionist Voice leader Jim Allister a 'thug' in a committee meeting. The DUP did their best to drag out the process, whereby the committee decided whether or not it would accept the findings of the commissioner, seeking legal advice and deferring a decision until a meeting on 20 May – which, conveniently, fell after the general elections on 7 May. Sammy Wilson was re-elected as MP for East Antrim; the committee report, which upheld the complaint against him, was finally published on 10 June.

Before the Assembly debate on a censure for Sammy Wilson, I sought advice from party colleagues as to whether I should speak out, using parliamentary privilege, about my perception of Jimmy Spratt's behaviour as chair of the Standards and Privileges Committee or even make a formal complaint against him. However, on the afternoon before the debate, Jimmy Spratt announced his resignation due to ill health. I thought it best to let it go.

However, Spratt was back for two more meetings of the Standards and Privileges Committee during September. At his final meeting, it seemed that he was exercising his last opportunity to get his pound of flesh as chair, venting comments about the commissioner even before the meeting began and continuing throughout the formal session. At one point, he tried to involve the Assembly legal advisor in his ridicule of the commissioner and embarrassed her, as she obviously did not wish to make any response. I was outraged and thought if I did not speak up I would be condoning his action. I raised my hand to speak.

'Chair, I understand you have a grievance against the Commissioner but you need to deal with it outside the committee as an individual MLA.' I added: 'Speaking against the commissioner the way you have done is not being impartial and objective as the chair of the committee.'

A hostile response followed – Spratt said I was challenging his authority as the chair and demanded I retract the remarks. When I declined, he stormed out of the room with a parting shot: 'Anna Lo, you will be hearing from my solicitor!' I never did.

I then had to chair the rest of the meeting myself, actually expecting the rest of the DUP members to walk out in support of him, which would mean that we would lose the quorum and be unable to continue with committee business. Thankfully they did not, but at the end of the meeting Robin Newton said that it was a pity that Jimmy Spratt's last committee meeting had ended this way. He proposed that the committee write a letter to acknowledge his contribution over the last year. We all agreed.

Although I did believe that we, as MLAs, should deal with the people we came across in a professional and respectful manner, I was no champion for the commissioner. In fact, I challenged Douglas Bain on his language and attitude towards two young women in the findings of his investigation of complaints of sexual harassment against Basil McCrea, published in March 2016, just before the end of the Assembly term. I accepted the ruling that McCrea had not breached any code of conduct, but reminded the commissioner that there was an imbalance of power between a male employer and young female employees on temporary contracts. I expressed my concerns about the fact that the accusations were dismissed on the grounds that they lacked collaborative evidence and that the complainants were perceived to be unreliable. I felt that this would send a message that would not encourage women to come forward to make such complaints in future.

Even with the revised code of conduct, the threshold for a breach of the code is high. The vast majority of complaints against MLAs is, therefore, deemed inadmissible. I recall a complaint made by Caitríona Ruane from Sinn Féin against the DUP's Jim Wells for breaching the code of respect in his manner towards a witness, Lucy Smith, during a Justice Committee meeting scrutinising the Human Trafficking Bill. I read the report of that meeting and was appalled by the hostile manner in which Ms Smith, who runs a website to improve the safety of sex workers, was questioned. The commissioner did not find a breach and, during the Standards and Privileges Committee meeting with him, I expressed my anger at the way Ms Smith had been treated. It was, in my view, brave of her to appear in front of the committee in a public session. Her testimony was, moreover, essential in presenting the perspective of the sector that would be directly affected – the bill in question proposed to ban prostitution in Northern Ireland. It was evident to me there was a lack of common decency, general respect and courtesy towards the witness, which should have been a breach of the desirable code of conduct of any elected representatives of the public. I asked whether Jim Wells would dare to use the same approach if he was questioning someone of a different profession.

Whilst all the parties accepted the code of conduct as reviewed and revised by the committee, there remains a glaring lack of transparency regarding donations to political parties in Northern Ireland. Although parties must report to the Electoral Commission details of donations they receive in the same way as parties in Great Britain, the commission in Northern Ireland is currently restricted to publishing only the overall figures, with no names and no statistical breakdown, on the grounds of security risks.

This secrecy has raised public concerns for a long time and led to the perception, rightly or wrongly, that big donors are able to exert undue influence on certain parties. It is long overdue that the proposed draft legislation be passed, allowing the commission to publish the names of donors who give more than £7,500. More transparency will undoubtedly help to improve public confidence in Northern Ireland's political parties.

18

Advocating Changing the Abortion Law

Abortion has been an emotive and controversial issue for Northern Ireland for many years. In April 2016, shortly after the dissolution of the Assembly, the Liberal Democrat peer David Steel, who was responsible for liberalising abortion law in Britain, said it was 'ridiculous' that Northern Ireland continued to operate under the 1861 legislation on abortion. He commented that, by not changing the law, politicians were discriminating against women, and urged the Assembly to come up 'at least to 1967, if not to 2016'. His criticism came after a twenty-one-year-old woman was given a suspended jail sentence – and thus a criminal record – at Belfast Crown Court for taking abortion pills she had bought online.

These were the most recent news headlines regarding the rights and wrongs of women having abortions in Northern Ireland. For years, local politicians have refused to extend the 1967 Abortion Act to Northern Ireland to bring it in line with the rest of the UK. This region has one of the strictest abortion laws in the world. We still operate under the archaic Offences Against the Person Act 1861, which decrees that abortion is only lawful if there is either a threat to the life of the mother or a risk of real and serious harm to her long-term or permanent health. The penalty for breaking the law can be as much as a life sentence.

Some people have called the 1967 Abortion Act 'abortion on demand'. That is inaccurate. The act simply extends the perimeter of defence for carrying out a termination up to twenty-four weeks under the same Offences Against the Person Act to include socio-economic factors such as the mother's age, economic circumstances and marital status, considered within the framework of women's health. It still needs the consent of two doctors.

I have always been pro-choice and make no apologies for it. I would like to see the Abortion Act introduced here to legalise abortions carried out up to twelve weeks. I believe this should be extended to twenty-four weeks for pregnancies with fatal foetal abnormality or resulting from sexual crime, since a medical diagnosis of abnormality may not be given until twenty weeks and sexual crime may involve legal processes.

I am of the strong view that no society that respects equality and individual autonomy should force a woman to continue with an unwanted pregnancy. Our restrictive laws do not prevent unplanned pregnancies; they only send women who are already under great emotional pressure to seek abortion outside of Northern Ireland, away from family support. Recent statistics show that an average of 1,075 residents of Northern Ireland travel to England to access termination services every year. This could well be an underestimate, as not all women give their address in Northern Ireland. Access to abortion in England is restricted to those Northern Irish women who can afford the cost of the procedure and travel – up to £2,000. Those on low incomes or on benefits have much more difficulty in coming up with that sort of money in a hurry; this can also lead to delays in accessing the termination. Therefore it is also a class issue. More and more people are being forced to take risks by purchasing abortion drugs online and administering them without medical supervision.

The hypocrisy of our politicians, mostly middle-aged males, turns my stomach. They prefer to export the problem than to show compassion and common sense and help women in the difficult circumstances of a crisis pregnancy. This is a health matter, not a criminal-justice issue. Women should not be criminalised for wanting to decide what to do with their bodies, nor for wanting to have children at the right time and under circumstances of their own choosing.

I suspect that my mother had one or two abortions in her life. My three older brothers, the sister who died in infancy and I were born in fairly quick succession. Henry was only eighteen months older than me; but between me and my sister, Mary, there is a gap of five years.

My mother had always been a very healthy woman who was hardly ever sick, but I remember one day she came home after being out with my aunt and went straight to bed. The adults whispered quietly and the children were told not to disturb Mother for a while. I was probably only about three or four years of age, but I remember being very anxious that she had suddenly taken ill. If she did have an abortion, it was a back-street one. My mother was lucky not to have been butchered and to have been able to give birth to my younger sister after that.

My mother loved us dearly and there was absolutely no

question of my parents not desiring more children. If they were forced to make that difficult decision it will have been because of their financial situation. At that time my father's shipping business had gone down the tubes and the family was in serious debt, living with our maternal grandparents in very crowded quarters. Could anyone blame my parents if they aborted their fifth child?

Here in Northern Ireland, women are not given the option of accessing a safe and free termination under the NHS like other women in the rest of the UK, because our politicians follow religious beliefs maintaining that life begins at conception and wish to protect the unborn child – who, in fact, has no status as a person under UK law. Research has shown that most abortions are conducted between 3 and 9 weeks' gestation and almost 90 per cent have been carried out by 12 weeks' gestation. In those early days, the foetus is merely a cluster of cells – not a thinking, reasoning, independent human being – and still very much a part of the woman's body. Yet, in Northern Ireland, women are prohibited by law from terminating its growth, even when the pregnancy is unplanned and unwanted.

When I was the head of the CWA, my interpreting staff helped to accompany a number of women, most of whom were illegal immigrants, to access abortions in Birmingham. These women had no choice, really. Owing to their lack of legal status, they could not register with a GP and would not be entitled to ante- or post-natal care, either in hospital or at home afterwards, under the NHS.

While I was a member of the Assembly, there were only four publicly declared pro-choice MLAs – me, Steven Agnew, Basil

McCrea and Dawn Purvis, who was in office from 2007 to 2011. I believe the politicians in Northern Ireland are out of step with the opinion of the majority of the population – particularly the younger generation, who wish to live in a more modern and liberal society. I recall a veteran politician from the SDLP giving me a piece of advice soon after I got elected as we sat beside each other in a coach to attend a conference. He said, 'Anna, you have a niche in politics and that's a good thing for any politician – but you must stop claiming to be pro-choice. That's going to lose you votes.' I appreciated his good intentions, but I had not been thinking only about gaining votes when I got into politics.

Soon after I became an MLA in 2007, I joined the advisory board of the Family Planning Association, which campaigns to try to bring the Abortion Act to Northern Ireland. They had persuaded the Labour MP Diane Abbott to submit an amendment to the Human Fertilisation and Embryology Bill in the autumn of 2008. The Family Planning Association sent facts and figures about abortions to MLAs to try to debunk myths. Dawn Purvis and I wrote to MPs to urge them to support the amendment to help give women in Northern Ireland the same rights as provided by the 1967 law. I have kept some replies, including those from Nick Clegg, the then-leader of the Liberal Democrats, and John Bercow, who was absolutely supportive of the proposed change. Dawn Purvis went to Westminster with supporters from Alliance for Choice to lobby MPs ahead of the debate.

Disappointingly, as a result of political pressure, the Labour government used a timetabling motion in the House of Commons debate, which effectively killed off a series of proposed amendments to the bill, including Diane Abbott's. We were all devastated as it was really the last chance to get the law extended here before criminal-justice powers were transferred to the Assembly later on that year. We knew it would be a huge uphill struggle, if not an impossible one, to amend the existing abortion law in Northern Ireland through the Assembly itself.

Extending the Abortion Act to Northern Ireland might be a big ask for our conservative politicians, but one might think that they could at least issue abortion guidelines for health-service staff. Yet the Family Planning Association has been in a fifteen-year battle to seek clarification on the abortion law for health professionals. In 2001 it sought a judicial review of the DHSS's failure to issue guidelines on when an abortion is legal in Northern Ireland. In 2004 the Court of Appeal ordered the department to draw up guidelines, but it was not until 2007 that draft guidelines were produced. However, the attempt was thwarted by the Assembly's Health Committee, led by Iris Robinson, which succeeded in having the guidelines rejected on moral grounds. New guidelines were issued a year later, but they faced a legal challenge from the Society for the Protection of the Unborn Child. Further revised guidelines were again published for consultation in 2010. It was frustrating and bewildering to witness the impediments that had been put in the way of attempts to clarify medical practices and enable our doctors and nurses to do their job. The anti-abortion lobby feared that the guidelines were a back door to bringing in 'abortion on demand'.

I had repeatedly asked questions in the Assembly regarding the progress of the guidelines and, following a meeting with a hospital consultant who expressed serious concerns about medical staff working without guidelines, written a feature piece about it for the *Belfast Telegraph*. The years of long delay had created a vacuum of clarity within the health service, leading to uncertainties for health professionals, who tended to err on the side of caution rather than to provide abortions in cases such as fatal foetal abnormality – which used to be done routinely, without any qualm. Their reluctance is, of course, understandable. If a health worker is judged to have carried out an illegal abortion, he or she could go to jail for life.

The abortion guidelines were eventually published on 25 March 2016, just days before the end of the Assembly term and twelve years after the court had ordered the Department of Health to produce them.

Incredibly, it took a brave woman's personal account to spark the recent momentum for change in the abortion law. There was a great deal of publicity in 2013 about the heartbreaking experience of Sarah Ewart, who had to go to England for an abortion when she found out that her baby had anencephaly, a malformation of the brain and skull that meant there was no chance that it would survive outside the womb. Sarah and her mum, Jane Christie, lobbied all the political parties, including my own. Meeting them in our team room face to face and hearing their upsetting story made us all resolve to try to get the law relaxed so that women in the same tragic circumstances as Sarah would not need to travel abroad for abortion in future.

True to his word, David Ford launched a consultation in 2014 and in 2015 sought agreement from the Executive to introduce legislative proposals to change the law on fatal foetal abnormality – but that was denied. Meanwhile, in a November 2015 judicial review sought by the Northern Ireland Human Rights Commission, the Northern Ireland High Court ruled that prohibition of abortion in cases of fatal foetal abnormality and sexual crime violated Article 8 of the European Convention on Human Rights. The court placed the onus on the Assembly to make the law compatible with human rights.

Without Executive agreement for David Ford's proposal, our only option was for Alliance backbench MLAs to submit amendments to the Justice (No. 2) Bill during its consideration stage. The party only aimed to effect change for fatal foetal abnormality, having reservations about the technicalities of proving sexual crime such as rape or incest. We believed that the amendment on fatal foetal abnormality might succeed if parties gave their members a free vote, but many doubted the chances of success for an amendment on sexual crime. It was agreed that the amendment on fatal foetal abnormality would be submitted in the names of Stewart Dickson, who was a member of the Justice Committee, and Trevor Lunn, the MLA for Lagan Valley. I asked for my name to be included, given my longstanding support for changing abortion law. However, I later decided to go it alone and put in an amendment on sexual crime. The party thought we should separate the two issues; thus, my name appeared on my own amendment only.

In drafting the amendment I consulted the Bill Office and other interested bodies, including a lawyer and a barrister in London who had been sympathetic to the campaign. I did not hold out much hope of gaining enough votes for the amendment to pass into the statute, but I thought it was essential to make a point. In fact, in a recent poll commissioned by Amnesty International, 66 per cent of those surveyed believed abortion should be allowed in the case of fatal foetal abnormality, while 69 per cent and 68 per cent respectively thought that the law in Northern Ireland should make access to abortion available where the pregnancy was the result of rape or incest. Steven Agnew from the Green Party and Basil McCrea of NI21 also jointly put in brief amendments on fatal foetal abnormality and sexual crime.

However, the DUP health minister, Simon Hamilton, announced out of the blue on the day of the debate that a working group would be established to review abortion legislation and would report back in the summer – again, conveniently, after the May elections. Many viewed this as kicking a difficult decision down the road to avoid controversy that might damage electoral success. It was a sneaky tactic to get the DUP off the hook for voting against the amendments on fatal foetal abnormality.

I was gearing myself up for a rowdy debate session, given the hostility I had received in a previous debate, when Paul Givan from the DUP had used an amendment to the Justice Bill to try to prevent private health clinics such as Marie Stopes from carrying out medical abortions in Northern Ireland. I had joined with Sinn Féin on that occasion to make up the numbers for a petition of concern to scupper his attempt.

The debate for our group of abortion amendments went on late into the night, but only one DUP speaker was picked to read her prepared speech. All the amendments failed, with the

DUP, the SDLP and most of the UUP voting against them.

However, I am hopeful that we have seen the start of a level of momentum we have never seen before, with more senior politicians than ever voicing their concerns. The outdated abortion law has been found by the judiciary to be incompatible with the European Convention on Human Rights and the Executive has been told it must remedy the provision of abortion, at least in cases of pregnancy with fatal foetal abnormality and resulting from sexual crime. The Court of Appeal has heard appeals from the Department of Justice and the attorney general on the judicial review on abortion rights, although no judgements have yet been announced. A Westminster peer, Lord Steel, has named and shamed politicians here as discriminating against women. The public has shown overwhelming support for change in these two areas. Politicians must act soon.

I believe that there is also momentum for change afoot in terms of rights for our lesbian, gay, bisexual and transsexual communities. The acceptance of equal marriage in both the rest of the UK and the Republic of Ireland has meant that Northern Ireland is yet again out of step with its neighbouring jurisdictions. Encouragingly, the current health minister, Michelle O'Neill, has abolished the ban on men who have had sex with men donating blood and brought this policy into line with the rest of the UK. Again, those politicians who oppose equal marriage will soon have to move with the tide of change.

19

The Flags Protests

My constituency manager, Councillor Catherine Curran, elected in 2011, was a breath of fresh air in Belfast City Council, bringing many new ideas and ample dynamism to the establishment. However, she got quite worried about a November 2012 motion about the flying of the union flag above the City Hall building. I was not particularly concerned, as I doubted anyone ever noticed it being flown at all. I was to be proven very wrong.

Sinn Féin had become the largest party in the council since the 2011 election and wanted either to remove the union flag or fly both the Irish and British flags together above the iconic seat of the Belfast local authority. Sinn Féin, supported by the SDLP, put forward a motion to council to stop flying the union flag. Colleagues in my party, which was the third-largest party in the council and held the balance of power between the nationalist and unionist blocs, proposed an amendment to fly the flag only on designated days, as was already the practice in the Northern Ireland Assembly and the unionist-dominated Craigavon and Lisburn Councils. This position of compromise had also been recommended by the Northern Ireland Equality Commission.

On 3 December 2012, the evening of the debate, the council passed the motion to fly the union flag only on designated days. The Alliance amendment was supported both by Sinn Féin and the SDLP, but not by any unionist councillors. This was the first time Sinn Féin and SDLP voted to support the flying of the flag on a council building, but not much attention was drawn to that fact.

However, weeks before the debate, the DUP, with the help of the UUP, had printed and distributed forty thousand leaflets throughout east Belfast. The leaflets were in Alliance colours and contained telephone numbers for our headquarters (where my office was also based) and the east-Belfast office. I was living in rented accommodation in the Knocknagoney area at the time and received one of the leaflets through my letterbox. It called on people to protest about the Alliance proposal and, I have no doubt, was intended to inflame tension and to attack the party ahead of the 2015 Westminster election.

And inflame tension it certainly did. Protests and riots erupted in Belfast city centre and other areas and continued for months, badly damaging trade in the city, not to mention Northern Ireland's international reputation. A couple of times, as I travelled from the city centre home to east Belfast, I met with protests on the streets, which could be quite scary. It saddened me to hear that many young Protestant men got criminal records as a consequence of these protests, which could damage their future employment and travel prospects. They were pawns being used in a political game.

Particular attention focused on Naomi Long, who had taken the Westminster seat from Peter Robinson in 2010. Anyone with a brain could see it made no sense to blame Naomi who, not being a local councillor, had had no role in the Belfast City Council decision. Nonetheless, she was made a scapegoat, encouraged by the DUP. Her constituency office was repeatedly attacked and she, personally, received death threats. Many other Alliance councillors and MLAs received threats too. Stewart Dickson's constituency office in Carrickfergus was burnt down and the home of two Bangor councillors, Christine and Michael Bower, was attacked, with their baby daughter inside.

I received threats, too, from people who claimed they knew where I lived. Yet again a police patrol started roaming the small private development in Knocknagoney where I was renting a house. At Christmas my son Conall and his partner, Fiona, visited me and could not help noticing the police presence on my street. A Sunday newspaper also received a bullet along with my picture and phoned me to ask if I wanted the story to be published. I declined, telling them there was no point in giving the bullies more media attention. Anyway, if they had wanted to shoot me they would have done it, rather than wasting a bullet in the post. In that moment I was more grateful than ever for my status as the only Chinese-born parliamentarian in Europe. Assassinating me would attract the worst kind of publicity to this corner of the continent. I did not think they would be foolish enough to try.

It was a worrying and testing time for all the public representatives from the party but, despite the turmoil, we knew we were right to put forward the proposal to keep the union flag flying on designated days and to try to achieve a compromise in a divided society. If anything, the furore stiffened our resolve to tackle the deep-seated divisions in Northern Ireland.

20

Cancer

Back in 2001, a friend who had not seen me for a while remarked that I had lost a lot of weight. I had not noticed this, but was aware that I had not been sleeping well and had lost my appetite. I went to see my doctor, who discovered that I was suffering from high blood pressure and gave me medication for it. I put it down to pressure at work and at home and thought it would be temporary. However, the condition persisted.

Soon after I became an MLA in May 2007, after a routine blood test in September in a new health clinic in the area I had moved to, a very experienced GP, Dr Darrah, called me one evening to ask me to see him first thing the next morning. I was not particularly worried and breezed in, praising him for his efficiency. However, he looked solemn and told me that my white-blood-cell count was abnormally high and that he needed to carry out some investigations. I remember asking him, 'What investigations? Do you mean cancer?'

'Yes,' he answered, gravely. It was hard to take in – I did not seem to have any symptoms of the disease.

A week later, I was at the Special Investigation Unit at the

Royal Victoria Hospital for a series of tests. I had an endoscopy in October, two days before I left for a conference at the University of Notre Dame in the USA, where I was to make a speech about racial equality in Northern Ireland. On arrival at the campus in Indiana, I lost my voice completely from laryngitis, possibly caused by the procedure. It was lucky that I just about got my voice back, although it was still hoarse, on the last day of the week-long conference, when I was due to speak. Mind you, I was feeling rather low, under the dark cloud of the investigation, and did not really enjoy the conference, even though I was able to meet the renowned human-rights lawyer and former president of Ireland, Mary Robinson, at the pre-conference reception and lecture.

Strangely, the results of the endoscopy found no sign of any cancer growth and the investigation was inconclusive. In the meantime I took a course of iron tablets to alleviate my anaemia. A couple of years later I went through a series of investigations all over again – blood tests were still indicating that my body was fighting against some kind of infection. However, once again, they failed to find anything. Crucially, I felt well and full of energy. I was not particularly concerned.

It was not until April 2012 that, after some more tests, a liver specialist in the Royal referred me to Dr Damien Finnegan in Belfast City Hospital for a bone-marrow test. This confirmed that I had basal-cell lymphoma, a low-grade non-Hodgkin lymphoma, which usually progresses slowly over a period of months or years in cells in the bone marrow. For this type of cancer, evidence suggests that no treatment is as good as treatment for people who are otherwise feeling well. Thus, luckily, I have so far been spared the side effects of chemotherapy. Instead, I am subject to a 'watch and wait' policy, being closely monitored until such time as the illness becomes worse. I receive regular check-ups from the very gentle and sensitive Dr Finnegan and the wonderful staff at Belfast City Hospital. I know, too, that I have to look after myself and keep healthy.

I suspect the cancer might even have been present back in 2001, when I suddenly lost weight and developed high blood pressure, which is an associated condition of the lymphoma. I have often wondered whether, if it had been diagnosed then, David and I would still have separated in June of that year.

The confirmation of cancer in 2012 could not have come at a worse time. I had just separated from Gavin and literally left the matrimonial home with a suitcase, moving from a luxury four-bedroom house in Jordanstown to a rented semi-detached house in a working-class area of east Belfast. My house off the Knocknagoney Road was a stone's throw away from a loyalist estate which had flags on nearly every lamp-post in July. I got some intimidation there. Shortly after I moved in, for example, I put up a side gate to block off access to the back of the property. Someone, for some unknown reason, kicked it open during the night; the bolt had to be reinforced. Needless to say, incidents like this did not help me as I tried to come to terms with my diagnosis.

I did not tell many people about the cancer. Indeed, as it never seemed imminent that I would be hampered by the illness, there was almost nothing to tell. I told my family, a couple of close friends and a few people in the Alliance Party; but I omitted to tell my close colleague, Catherine Curran, in my constituency office. It was only a year later that I happened to mention it to her. She burst into tears when she heard the news.

There was no point in wallowing in self-pity. I had to get on with getting over the marriage breakup and fulfilling my role in the Assembly. Perhaps my tough Chinese roots kept me going. I was thankful that I had a busy, full-time job that absorbed all my time and focus.

21

European Election, 2014

The Alliance Party leadership wanted someone high profile to kick off the season of elections. They wanted an impressive result in the European election in May 2014 so as to pave the way for the contest to retain Naomi Long's Westminster seat in the general election in 2015, a match we anticipated that the DUP would fight tooth and nail after the humiliation Peter Robinson, then first minister, had suffered when Naomi unseated him in 2010.

David Ford, Naomi Long and Stephen Farry took three months to persuade me to stand for the European election. I was a most reluctant candidate, for personal reasons as well as political ones. Firstly, although I wholeheartedly supported the UK's membership of the EU, I knew hardly anything about European politics and certainly had never had any ambition to be an MEP. Given the slim chance of Alliance winning one of the three seats in Europe, I argued it was better to field someone new – someone who could use the opportunity to gain some publicity and raise their profile for future elections. It would not have any effect on my electability. I had already decided to stand down at the end of my second term in 2016.

The personal reasons might not have been too obvious to the party. Even though I had been granted a divorce uncontested, I was embroiled in a legal dispute with my former husband over the financial settlement. The dispute had been dragging on for over a year, causing me a lot of distress and anger, never mind legal fees. I was also conscious of my state of health following the diagnosis of lymphoma, which could worsen at any time. I was already overtired; electioneering on top of my usual workload in the Assembly would not do my health any favours.

In February, Naomi and Stephen came to plead with me again. Naomi apologised for their persistence, saying she was embarrassed to have to ask me again and again. It was difficult to refuse two people I highly admired and respected, even though I did not always agree with them on every issue. I relented, perhaps against my better judgement. David Ford gave me his guarantee that I would get as much support as I required and that there would be no strenuous canvassing throughout the region. The party announced my nomination on 5 February and, true to their promise, provided me with a mountain of information on Europe, which I duly memorised and regurgitated in hustings. From mid-April until polling day on 22 May it was all go – hustings, media interviews and knocking on doors (mostly in Belfast). All the while I was continuing to work full time in the Assembly.

Something more exciting was also scheduled for that May. The prestigious Giro d'Italia cycle race, one of the great sporting events of Europe, which would be watched by millions of viewers worldwide, was to pass through Northern Ireland from 9 to 11

May. It was a great coup for Northern Ireland to win the right to host the event, which would no doubt boost our tourism and economy. Mark H. Durkan, the environment minister, requested and received all-party support to ban EU election posters on lamp-posts along the three cycle routes – in Belfast, along the Antrim coast and on the road between Armagh and Dublin. Meanwhile, Nelson McCausland of the DUP, the minister for social development, made money available for towns along the route to improve the appearance of derelict buildings and other eyesores.

In the same vein, I weighed in, releasing a statement calling for the removal of flags flying on lamp-posts, many of which were tattered, and suggesting that the paramilitary murals with intimidating portrayals of hooded gunmen along the routes should be painted over, thus providing a new and positive image of Northern Ireland for the world to see. However, the DUP was quick to attack me, with Sammy Wilson describing any suggestions of removing union flags from lamp-posts as 'folly' and claiming that such a move could spark civil disorder.

Sadly, I received a barrage of racist abuse on Facebook and Twitter. Some of it was not only hurtful but also intimidating. There were, for example, several posts showing a person holding a machine gun (later found to be an imitation) along with my election poster and threatening messages. I was glad that the police took swift action to investigate the online abuse and actually got results, unlike the time of my first election, when they had seemed powerless. A number of people received police warnings and one person was found guilty of a number of counts of 'improper use of public electronic communications network' and given suspended sentences.

I was grateful to Kate Nicholl, my parliamentary assistant, and to my colleague Stewart Dickson, the party chief whip, who tried their best to shield me from what was being said. They knew how much I had going on in my life on top of the pressure of running for the European parliament. They took screenshots of the worst comments and reported them to the police. I read some of them after the election and was totally disgusted by the vile and racist insults that had been flung at me. I could accept rational objections to my call for the removal of flags and murals along the routes, but personal attacks using foul and degrading language made me feel angry. It was sad that some people would stoop so low as to make depraved, demeaning comments in order to hurt another person.

However, following media reports of the online abuse, I was overwhelmed with gratitude for the thousands of goodwill messages sent to me in emails, telephone calls, letters and visits to my office, as well as in social-media posts using the hashtag '#IStandWithAnna'. It was heartening to hear from so many people who felt compelled to express their disgust at the racist comments and agreed with my sensible proposal to remove flags and paramilitary murals from the Giro route. The positive responses totally outweighed the tiny minority of people who sought to voice their views in a negative fashion. I felt proud that so many people in Northern Ireland would stand up against racism.

The first and deputy first minister, as well as other politicians, united to condemn the abuse directed at me too. The then-deputy prime minister, Nick Clegg, even phoned me to offer his support. On that occasion I was in a fairly fractious meeting with local residents in the Village area, discussing a proposed regeneration plan with Housing Executive officials. There were drawings spread all over the table and a robust exchange of questions and answers was in full swing. When the meeting was over I switched my phone back on; it rang. It was the deputy PM, out of the blue and utterly unexpected. Lots of people were still standing around, gathering their papers and talking, and I was quite distracted by the background noise in the room. It was both funny and embarrassing when he said, 'Hello, this is Nick Clegg ...' and I shouted, 'Sorry, Nick who?' I am quite sure I sounded baffled and incoherent to Mr Clegg. When I got back to my office, my staff said I was behaving like an overexcited schoolgirl, yelling, 'I was speaking to Nick Clegg!' They had been frantically trying to contact me to alert me that he was going to call after my meeting, but I did not receive the warning in time to recognise him on the phone.

It was still weeks until polling day and, little did I know, I had far more publicity coming my way. In researching this book I have been dreading having to reread the newspaper articles and to relive the horror and stress I went through after making comments in an interview with John Manley of the *Irish News* regarding my 'aspiration' for a united Ireland. In that interview I expressed the view that a thirty-two-county state would be 'better placed economically, socially and politically' and that it was 'very artificial' to divide up the island of Ireland and to make one corner of it part of the United Kingdom.

The press and the television coverage over my remarks went on for days– in their view Alliance was supposed to be a 'soft' unionist party. With only just eight weeks before the May elections, the commentators described my 'revelation' as 'setting the cat amongst the pigeons' within the party and declared that it would give unionist parties another stick to beat us with. The dust had only just settled after we were blamed for the removal of the union flag from Belfast City Hall. I often wonder if there would have been such a reaction if I had said I supported remaining part of the UK.

The interview with John Manley was bad timing. I had been away with the Standards and Privileges Committee to Washington and Maryland for several days on a fact-finding visit. I was to learn more about the USA's lobbying legislation and best practice and inform the committee, which would help with the task of revising the Assembly code of conduct. I came back on Sunday, 16 March and worked flat out at home throughout Saint Patrick's Day, going through nearly 120 amendments submitted by all parties for the consideration stage of the extensive Local Government Bill. As the Environment Committee chair and Alliance representative, I was responsible for commenting on the amendments in the extended debates scheduled over the next two days from Tuesday in the Assembly. I was still jetlagged.

The interview with the *Irish News* had taken place in my office in the presence of the Alliance press officer on Tuesday lunchtime, in between the debates, and had lasted for almost forty minutes. During that time I had answered John Manley's list of prepared questions about the Alliance Party, the Assembly and the European elections. It was towards the end of the interview that John had asked me my view on the constitutional issue. I had set out the Alliance policy supporting the principle of consent enshrined in the Good Friday Agreement – that a united Ireland would only come into being if it were the wish of the majority of the people in Northern Ireland. I had gone on to say that, personally, I would like to see a united Ireland, but that it may not happen in my lifetime. I should have stopped there – I have no idea why I went on to talk about the border being artificial and my anti-colonial views. I can only put it down to John's very skilful interviewing techniques and my own naïveté.

I was flabbergasted by the media storm raised by my remarks. I was a known liberal with a more progressive perspective than some other politicians in the Assembly, and this was not the first time I had spoken in public both about my support for a united Ireland as a long-term vision and my distaste for colonialism from my personal experience of growing up in a British colony. My opinions had never raised any eyebrows before.

My main concerns, now, were for my party colleagues fighting for their seats on local councils. Those elections were due to take place at the same time as the European ones in May. I was consumed with worry that my remarks had jeopardised their chances. Trevor Lunn was confronted by one long-term Alliance voter who said that she would never vote for him again and that the Alliance Party should send me packing on a one-way ticket back to Hong Kong! I could understand party colleagues' concerns and I blamed nobody but myself. I hardly slept for nights. I thought about resigning but I knew that would only make it worse.

However, the party united behind me with unfailing support – something I will always remember and be grateful for. Shortly after the media storm and, as usual, some racist social-media reactions, I made a speech at the Alliance Party Conference, making it clear that I refused to be reduced to one label, just as the Alliance Party cannot be reduced to the labels of nationalist or unionist. I highlighted that Alliance is a cross-community party (something the media seemed not to comprehend) that champions and cherishes diversity. I pointed out that what saddened me was that the focus on my comments reflected that there were those, with their orange and green lenses, who were incapable of seeing beyond sectarianism. I ended by saying, 'Don't call me "nationalist"; don't call me "unionist". Call me "for everyone". Call me "Alliance".' To my surprise and great delight I received a standing ovation.

A week before the European elections, my sister, Mary, came over to visit Henry and me for ten days. Mary is now a very successful businesswoman and runs a multi-million-pound company with her husband in Hong Kong and China. I managed to see her a few times and showed her my new home. On polling day, my office suggested I take the day off, as there was not much more I could do. We went to Mount Stewart, which absolutely delighted Mary, who loved the gardens. She was due to depart the following day and, by way of a break from the election count, I arranged to have *dim-sum* lunch with her and Henry in south Belfast before she left. Beforehand, I went to a Belfast department store to look for a gift for her and got a lovely Belleek picture-frame. Unfortunately, I was spotted by a journalist, who tweeted and wrote in his newspaper the next day that I had gone out shopping on the crucial counting day.

It was hard to know whether the flags issue and my remarks on a united Ireland made any difference to the party votes in the local-government elections, since local council boundaries had been redrawn. However, I received the best result ever for the party in any European elections, with over 44,000 votes and 7.1 per cent of the total vote share.

Although I did not win a seat, I was pleased with the result and relieved that I had delivered the goal the party had been aiming for. However, I was truly glad to see the end of that campaign, which reinforced my decision not to stand in another election ever again. Politics is not for the faint hearted.

22

Dealings with Pastor McConnell and Peter Robinson

One evening in 2014, not long after I moved into my own home, a bungalow in a quiet area of north Down, I received a phone call from the police. The caller identified himself as a constable from the Bangor police station and told me they needed to see me urgently, adding, 'We are on our way, only twenty minutes away. Don't open the door to anyone until we arrive.'

It sounded pretty ominous. Anticipating another threat, I called Henry to ask if I could stay with him in case there was a serious problem that might necessitate my leaving home immediately. And of course, my dear brother said, 'No problem. There's always a room here for you!'

Two PSNI officers arrived and duly warned me that there had been another threat against me. I surmised it was something to do with comments I had made in a radio interview, condemning paramilitary activities. The officers assured me there would again be a regular police patrol on my street to give me some protection but stressed that I needed to take personal precautions. Two crime-prevention officers also came to advise me on stepping up security measures around the property.

By now, every time I moved to a new home, a new threat followed. My sons, Conall and Owen, were naturally concerned and we had discussed whether I should move to England to be near them and escape from these shadows of threat. I dismissed the perceived risks – not only because I wanted to carry on with my political role in Northern Ireland, but also because I knew that they came from a very small minority, most of whom were cowards and bullies who, like all cowards and bullies, used such tactics to intimidate and silence people who had a different view from them. I was not going to let them win.

However, I was getting increasingly alarmed by the escalation in attacks on immigrants over the previous six months. There were by then on average two to three incidents reported daily to the police, although that was not the full picture, as some people did not contact the PSNI for a number of reasons, including fear of reprisals. There were also some worrying new trends. Racist incidents used to be mostly confined to certain areas of south Belfast where new immigrants had availed of cheap rental properties, but these recent attacks were now occurring across the city. While it used to be mostly verbal abuse or low-level harassment, many recent incidents involved vicious physical attacks on properties and individuals. A Polish woman told me in tears that, after several incidents near where she lived in Sydenham, her family had moved to the back of their house and moved their baby's cot away from the upstairs bedroom window for fear of becoming victims of another racist attack. They wanted to move out of east Belfast but did not know where would be safe for them and their young children.

Earlier in the year, the assistant chief constable, Will Kerr, had commented that racist crimes within certain areas of the city had 'a deeply unpleasant taste of a bit of ethnic cleansing' about them. As the founder and the chair at the time of the Assembly All-Party Group on Ethnic Minorities, I sought the views of the community groups who were involved in promoting community relations on the ground. I was told that, with government cutbacks, there were very limited resources to continue with such projects. Representatives from ethnic-minority communities also expressed not just nervousness at the rising tide of racism in Northern Ireland, but also frustration at the seven-year delay to the publication of the revised Racial Equality Strategy, which had created a vacuum for the authorities in dealing with racial tension and inequality.

One Thursday, on my way from Stormont to my constituency office after a committee meeting, I stopped in Connswater Shopping Centre to get a picture taken for a new passport. On my way out of the centre to the front car park, I heard people shouting my name. As they did not sound particularly friendly, I quickened my pace and got to where my car was parked. Then a car passed me. A young woman was practically hanging out of the back passenger window, screaming abuse at me. I was extremely glad that they did not catch up with me and that there was a barrier between the road where the vehicle was travelling and my car. I was quite sure that, if they had got closer to me, there would have been an ugly scene. It brought back a nasty experience I had had in the 1970s, when a group of punks had verbally abused and assaulted me in Belfast city centre in broad daylight. When I got back to my office, I was a bit shaken.

Soon after that, in a Sunday sermon in May, which was also broadcast on the internet, a hard-line evangelical pastor named James McConnell described the Islamic faith as 'heathen', 'satanic' and 'a doctrine spawned in hell'. He remarked that he did not trust Muslims and called Enoch Powell 'a prophet' for predicting that immigration would bring rivers of blood.

I was astounded by the comments, which were echoed by a couple of other church ministers. I was even more astounded when the then-health minister, Edwin Poots, and other elected DUP representatives expressed public support for the preacher. However, I was utterly incensed and disgusted when Peter Robinson, then first minister of Northern Ireland, made comments in defence of the pastor. He added fuel to the fire by stating that he would not trust Muslims involved in terrorism or devoted to Sharia law, but would trust Muslims to 'go down to the shop' for him and to give him 'the right change'. It caused a media storm, with various political parties and commentators condemning his remarks as unacceptable.

I watched *The Nolan Show* on television in horror – in it, McConnell reiterated his offensive views and thanked Robinson for his support. I felt ashamed for Northern Ireland. I thought that they had made us a worldwide laughing stock.

However, what caused me more dismay was that, given the already-rising number of racist incidents, this row was very likely to incite more hatred against ethnic-minority people, leading to yet more attacks on already vulnerable and frightened immigrant communities. Robinson's remarks were demeaning, negatively stereotyping a whole community – which amounts to being racist and certainly does not befit the first minister of the region. His reference to Muslims as being messengers and shopkeepers showed his utter ignorance of the diversity of the four-thousand-strong Muslim community, which makes significant contributions to our society in many different fields, particularly in the health service. His remarks had damaged community relations and could potentially harm our capacity to attract inward investment and tourism from Muslim countries. Any mainstream politician in the rest of the UK would have been sacked right away; many had stood down for much less.

The *Guardian* interviewed me the morning after *The Nolan Show* was broadcast, and I hit out at the outrageous comments made by both the preacher and Peter Robinson. The Belfast correspondent then asked me if I would seek re-election in 2016. I confirmed that I would not. Next, I went on Stephen Nolan's radio programme and, when the presenter pressed me on racism against me particularly, I became a bit emotional. The BBC television evening news carried out an interview with me that same afternoon, in which I called for Robinson to apologise and retract his words. I explained my frustration with the current situation – the recent spike in racist attacks, the lack of resources for work on the ground and the seven-year delay in the publication of the revised Racial Equality Strategy. What made me particularly angry, I added, was that when the pastor made such unacceptable comments about the Muslim community we had politician after politician from the DUP voicing support for him, including the first minister. I then asked, 'What sort of place are we now living in?' I became tearful, admitting that I felt vulnerable walking along the street because I knew that ethnic-minority residents were being picked on daily. Some were considering leaving and I, too, was beginning to reflect on the idea.

To be honest, I was quite embarrassed afterwards at not being able to control my emotions and letting my sense of vulnerability show. However, letting down my guard had somehow aroused some positive reactions.

Over the next few days, there were thousands of messages of support, particularly under the Twitter hashtag '#IStandWith Anna'. By the end of the week, my constituency office resembled a florist's shop, with over a dozen bouquets of flowers delivered there. I was overwhelmed by the messages from well-wishers, some of which moved me to tears.

Thanks to twenty-four-year-old Lorcan Mullen from Strabane and other organisers, an anti-racism rally was held within days in Belfast city centre, at which four thousand people turned up. Lorcan told a newspaper that seeing me break down had been a tipping point for him, which had led him to organise the rally so that people could stand up against racism, xenophobia and Islamophobia. It was a glorious day at the end of May with the sun shining on our faces. Young people and old people, white people and people of colour, came together from different parts of Northern Ireland. There was almost a carnival atmosphere, with people holding homemade placards, one of which I particularly loved. It carried the words, 'Don't Go, Anna Lo!' surrounded by red hearts. Many people stood up on a small makeshift stand

and spoke passionately. I told the crowd that their support had restored my faith in the good people of Northern Ireland and I was determined to stay put. Many people called for a public apology from Peter Robinson.

Dozens also used humour to make their point by joining a flashmob protest outside the Tesco store on Royal Avenue, holding posters saying, 'I am shopping for Peter' – to the delight of hundreds of onlookers.

A similar anti-racism rally was also held in Derry-Londonderry, with almost a hundred supporters, including the environment minister, Mark H. Durkan, and the mayor of Derry, Martin Reilly.

A week afterwards, another rally organised by Amnesty International, the Northern Ireland Committee of the Irish Congress of Trade Unions and the Northern Ireland Council for Ethnic Minorities was also attended by thousands of people in Belfast city centre.

I was heartened, of course, by the outpouring of support for me but, more than that, I was elated that so many people had taken a stand against racism. It was gratifying for campaigners like me to see the positive impact of years of work promoting race relations. Here was proof that many people in Northern Ireland wanted a pluralist and inclusive society for all.

It was people power, really, that eventually forced Peter Robinson to make a public apology after a visit to the Belfast Islamic Centre on 3 June. Shortly after that OFMDFM published a draft Racial Equality Strategy for consultation.

Quite rightly, Pastor McConnell was prosecuted for making

offensive comments. In January 2016, the court decided that, while his comments had been offensive, they had not reached the 'grossly offensive' threshold required by law for a criminal conviction. He was therefore acquitted.

Looking back, at that time I was in deep despair and fearful that we were on a downward slope towards unprecedented violence against ethnic minorities. However, even in my darkest hours, light always came from the people in Northern Ireland, the vast majority of whom are always unequivocal in condemning racism. I am proud to be a member of the population here and have banished the thought of leaving. This is my home.

23

Retirement

I stepped down from formal politics at the end of the last Assembly term on 29 March 2016, after serving as an MLA for South Belfast for nine years. It was a huge privilege and an honour to represent the constituency and to highlight issues in the Northern Ireland Assembly.

The Alliance Party discovered my potential to shine as a public representative and provided me with their unfailing support throughout my tenure, during both good times and difficult times. I am grateful for their trust in me and will continue to be an active member of the party, although no longer in frontline politics. The party has been like a big family to me and I have made many lifelong friends from the ranks of its members and colleagues.

During canvassing for my party for the fresh Assembly elections in May 2016, many constituents were complimentary about my work and greeted me with great warmth. Some expressed their disappointment that I was not standing again and wanted to know my reason for leaving politics.

The simple answer is that I have worked for most of my life, since I was seventeen years of age, with just a few years' time out for child-rearing and full-time studies. At the age of sixty-five, it is probably time for me to retire. Fortunately, I am still in good health and, if I had the inclination, I could probably have gone on for another term. After all, there is no upper age limit for a politician – Ian Paisley Senior was a case in point.

However, politics is a tough and all-consuming profession. The turbulent events of the last few years confirmed to me that it was time to go and let new, young, fresh blood take on the challenge of trying to make Northern Ireland a better place.

I went into politics in 2007, after some years of direct rule. There was certainly great optimism at the time for a new dawn in this troubled land and I wanted to play a role in achieving a better and shared future for all. The first mandate got parties around the table, but it was frustrating that delivery of policies and public services was slow.

The second mandate, beginning in 2011, made some progress. In fact, the number of laws the Assembly produced in those five years compared not too badly with the other devolved regions of the UK. Inward investment increased, bringing more job opportunities, and crime went down; but the economy still lagged behind the rest of the UK. Although there has been improvement in recent years, we continue to have the highest economic inactivity and the highest youth unemployment in the UK, and our society is still deeply divided, with continued segregation in education, housing and some aspects of civic society. There is no clear and united political leadership on promoting reconciliation or dealing with issues of the past, victims and survivors. The so-called 'culture war' is continuously played out over flags, parades, paramilitaries and the Irish and Ulster-Scots languages and cultures. The cost of division in the duplication of services, in security and in missed opportunities is draining our resources. The continuing brain-drain of our smartest young people is economically and socially unsustainable, particularly for a society that needs to rebuild itself after years of conflict and destruction.

It is evident from the last two Assembly mandates that there is little trust between the two major parties, the DUP and Sinn Féin, which dominate the Executive. It would appear that, when they are not engaged in the sectarian carve-up of power, they tend to be at loggerheads with each other. There have been unacceptable delays in agreeing and producing policies and releasing available funds because of opposing ideologies and lack of goodwill between the two main parties. They have procrastinated about making decisions or wasted time vetoing each other. The closing years of the last Assembly saw Stormont lurch from crisis to crisis.

By the summer of 2015 I was quite fed up with the dysfunctional working of the bickering Executive, which was always close to collapsing the institutions. I considered resigning and co-opting someone with aspirations of becoming an MLA to take over for several months from September to March, then to stand in his or her own right in May 2016. However, with another crisis looming, I was told by party activists to stay put, as it would be unlikely that anyone would wish to step into my position only to find himself or herself out of a job within months.

I was glad I stayed until the end. It was good to see the Assembly stabilising somewhat and lovely to have the opportunity to say goodbye to colleagues and staff in the party as well as in the Assembly at the end of its natural term. They had all given me enormous support; I could not have functioned effectively without them.

On reflection, I believe I made some difference in the Assembly that hopefully will benefit our society as a whole. Naturally, as the first MLA with a minority-ethnic background, I championed assiduously the need to tackle racial inequality and racism in Northern Ireland. Thankfully, we now have the revised Racial Equality Strategy, the Ethnic Minority Development Fund to support the work of organisations and the flourishing All-Party Group on Ethnic Minority Communities, which I set up.

Human trafficking is an issue I brought to public attention before entering politics and I continued to raise awareness from within the Assembly. It is gratifying that now there is legislation as well as support and facilities for victims of this heinous crime. They are no longer regarded as illegal immigrants to be deported as soon as possible. A friend in the Law Centre recently remarked that I played a significant role in calling attention to the problem and lobbying for change.

A fellow committee member, Alban Maginness, once said that I had injected passion about environmental issues into the Environment Committee. I care deeply about the protection of our wildlife, our natural heritage and our built heritage and hope that the new Department of Agriculture, Environment and Rural Affairs will continue to have the environment high on its agenda, including continuing to host the annual Environment Week.

Despite often being a lone voice in the Assembly in advocating for the extension of the Abortion Act 1967 to Northern Ireland, I believe that momentum for change is gathering and I am optimistic that some flexibility for women facing unplanned or crisis pregnancies will follow. The long-awaited abortion guidelines for health professionals have at long last been published.

Equality for the LGBT community has always been close to my heart and I consistently voted in favour of equal marriage. I believe the Assembly will soon have to fall in line with other jurisdictions in legalising it.

I also unequivocally supported women's rights and gender equality in Northern Ireland over the years and was particularly delighted that the Women's Fund, of which I am an ambassador, organised a farewell lunch for me in the Members' Dining Room. I made many friends in that sector.

I hope it will not be too long before there is more 'normal' politics in the Assembly than the divisive 'identity politics' of orange and green. We need more young people, especially women, who are well educated and capable to enter politics and to replace the old and tired rhetoric of 'us' and 'them' with fresh ideas that will improve life for everyone in Northern Ireland.

On reflection, I am satisfied with my life's direction of travel so far and I think my parents would have been proud of me. I have no regrets about leaving Hong Kong, even though it has meant that family connections have been difficult to maintain. But we all have only one life to live and, whilst I might have missed some opportunities in Hong Kong, other wonderful doors have opened for me here in Northern Ireland.

I have always been driven to improve myself and I can proudly say that my career has been a fruitful journey of lifelong learning. It was hard and lonely at the beginning to learn and adapt to a new culture and environment, but with time and determination I have not only integrated but also challenged the status quo in this, my adoptive country. I love Northern Ireland, I love its people and I have put down my roots here. It is the place I call home.

My twenty-six-year marriage to David, despite its ups and downs, brought me the greatest joys of my life – my two wonderful sons, who were a pleasure to bring up and never fail to make me proud of their talents, achievements, strong social conscience and support for me. Henry and I attended the fabulous wedding of Conall and Fiona in July 2016 in Oxford, where Fiona is an associate professor. Conall is returning to work in public health in January after completing his PhD. Owen, a talented architect now based in London, was the best man at his brother's wedding.

My brief second marriage, despite the trauma and grief, taught me a lot about myself and the need for resilience. As for life after two divorces and retirement, I am very content to be on my own. I value my independence and the freedom to do what I want at my own pace and in my own time, without having to compromise with anyone else. It is great to have a circle of really good friends with whom I enjoy going out to cinemas, to theatres, to concerts and on walks.

I look forward to devoting time to voluntary work with NGOs in the environment, arts and ethnic-minority sectors and to offer them any help I can give from the experience I gained in government, and from campaigning and challenging inequalities.

I am sure they will keep me on my toes. I have taken up gardening and my garden has never looked so well. I may even take up painting again and develop a new career. You never know.

Acknowledgements

Since hearing about my great-grandfather's adventure from an uncle in 2008, I have wanted to write about my life and my family's journeys. I met Helen Wright last year at a friend's book launch and she was very enthusiastic about the idea. I wish to express my gratitude to Helen and to Patsy Horton of Blackstaff Press for their encouragement and guidance in making the thought a reality and to Alicia McAuley for fine-tuning the text. I wish to thank Kate Nicholl for her assistance in collating background material and proofreading the first draft. I am grateful to my sons, Conall and Owen, for their willingness to share their stories in my book. There were others whom I consulted about sections of the book and I am grateful for helpful comments from Brice Dickson, Paul Hainsworth, Deborah Gadd, Stephen Farry and Gordon Kennedy.